MATH TIME

The Learning Environment

Kathy Richardson

Educational Enrichment, Inc.
Norman, Oklahoma

Math Time™ **is a trademark of Educational Enrichment, Inc.**
Unifix® **is an exclusive design manufactured in Great Britain by**
Philip & Tracy, Ltd. It is distributed in the USA by
Didax Educational Resources, Peabody, Massachusetts.

Art Direction, Design & Layout:	F/X International Design
Production and Coordination:	Sheryl Russell
Editing:	Karen Antell
Illustration Coordinator:	Janann Roodzant
Illustrations:	Linda Starr
Children's Work:	Terrace Park School,
	Edmonds School District,
	Edmonds, WA.
	Colleen Gidner, Teacher

Printed in the United States of America

Published by
Educational Enrichment, Inc.
770 W. Rock Creek Road
P.O. Box 1524
Norman, Oklahoma 73070

Math Time workshops, videotapes and other related resources by
Kathy Richardson are available from Educational Enrichment, Inc.
For information call: (800) 292-6022.

Table of Contents

ii

Acknowledgements

Writing this book caused me to take a journey back through time as I reflected on all my years in the classroom. I remember so clearly that first year of teaching, when I had 36 children in my first grade room. What a challenging year that was, with nothing quite the way I had imagined it when I was taking college classes. I hope my children learned something that year; I know I did.

It's funny what you remember. My first week of teaching is forever imprinted in my mind. There was Donnie who cried because he didn't have his money for ice cream. I wasn't sure I knew what to do if someone had stolen his nickel, but when I asked what had happened, he tearfully confessed he had swallowed it. And I remember the lunch box dripping white foamy liquid and Tammi's disappointment that the ice cream bar she had saved to eat after school had melted. I also remember my first day teaching kindergarten, when all I said was, "I need some helpers to pass out the milk," and I ended up with 33 children in my lap. It was those little unexpected things that often got in the way of the work I was trying so hard to do.

I remember the other kinds of problems as well — the problems that arose because I didn't know how to make mathematics meaningful to my children. I remember Marie, strong and tall and so confident on the playground. But Marie had no confidence in her ability to make sense of the math we were doing. That was very clear to me one day when I asked what I thought was an obvious question: "Is the orange rod longer or shorter than the yellow rod?" The evidence was in front of her, but she didn't know. She was looking for the trick, the right answer, the clue on my face.

And I never will forget Joey. One day, he was the first one done with his worksheet — because he had written "1" as the answer for every problem on the page. When I impatiently asked, "Joey, what are you doing?", he looked up at me and said, "Why you always mad to me, teacher?" I knew I wasn't "mad to" Joey. But I was frustrated with my own teaching and not knowing how to help him. Why was mathematics so hard for my children? They seemed to know how to do something one day and then forget it the next day. There was a level of frustration and confusion in my children that was intolerable to me. And even more intolerable was the attitude, "I don't want to understand. Just show me what to do."

This wasn't the way it was supposed to be. There were many times when all I could see were the problems. How could I ever meet all the needs that presented themselves to me? How could I create a positive, effective classroom where we were all glad to come each day to spend precious time together? As the years passed, I kept searching for ways to help my children make sense of the work they were asked to do. What most changed my life as a classroom teacher was meeting and working with Mary Baratta-Lorton. She was the first person who not only understood my questions, but helped me figure out some answers as well. Through my work with Mary, I found we could help children make sense of mathematics. We could meet the range of needs in our classroom. We could teach and the children could learn — with joy and enthusiasm.

I have had lots of opportunities to learn during my life as a teacher. First of all, the children taught me what really matters. But I could not have grown as a teacher if it were not for the grown-ups in my life who were always willing to listen and try to help me figure this out. During those early years in the classroom, Janann Roodzant, Agnes Hinojos, Norma Gonné, Concha Cesena, and Laura Sanchez were always there to lend a hand and help me keep my perspective. Margie Gonzales, Deane Reed, Leslie Salkeld, Jody Walmsley, and Mary Baratta-Lorton made me believe my endless questions were interesting and even important. Later, Deborah Kitchens, Ruth Parker, Linda Gregg, Pat Sherbondy and Chris Oster were there to challenge my thinking, ask me questions, and give me feedback as I worked to communicate what I had learned. I thank them *all* for their love, support, wisdom, and encouragement.

Much of what I know I learned the hard way, by finding out what doesn't work as well as what does. I hope the information in this book will help some of you avoid the mistakes I made and stay focused on what really matters. We have an awesome responsibility as we work to find ways to create a learning environment that truly supports the children we are there to serve. This book is dedicated to all the children and all the teachers who lived and learned with me and to all the teachers who continue to find ways to support children as they grow and learn.

Preface

This is a book that honors and celebrates the way young children learn. It is based on the belief that we can maximize children's learning if we look honestly and respectfully at their way of working and establish an environment that is consistent with how they learn. Children are very good at learning to say words or follow procedures before they understand them. Too often we make assumptions about what children really know and understand, and in the process, we ignore their real needs. We often expect either too much or not enough. However, children thrive in an environment that supports them in their search for sense and meaning and provides them with basic concepts and understandings that help build a strong foundation for the learning they will do in the future. The more we know and understand about the real work of the young child, the more we will be able to create a positive learning environment that provides them with appropriate challenges and expectations.

All teachers bring the goals and objectives of their math programs to life as they plan and present activities, establish procedures and expectations, and interact with children. Teachers' beliefs about what children need to know, their knowledge of how children learn, and the classroom environment they create all impact how children experience mathematics.

How children experience mathematics has a profound effect on ***what*** they are able to learn. If we want our children to be successful in mathematics, it is vitally important that we create a learning environment that supports the development of understanding. If children learn mathematics in a way that allows them to understand what they are learning, they learn that mathematics makes sense and learn to trust their own abilities to make sense of it. The ability to do mathematics well develops in children as they learn to see relationships and to make connections. On the other hand, children who learn merely to follow procedures to get correct answers will not trust their own ability to make sense of mathematics. They will not look for relationships and will not be able to apply what they know in new situations. The mathematics they learn will serve them in very limited ways.

Those of us who work with young children know how important the early years are for building a base for all subsequent mathematical learning. For children to be successful in mathematics beyond the primary grades, they must leave with more than knowledge. They must also develop positive attitudes and habits of mind that cause them to be interested, curious, and eager to learn new mathematical ideas. Children need to see mathematics as something that is useful to them when they solve problems or make decisions. ***Math Time: The Learning Environment*** was written to help teachers of primary children establish a classroom that is supportive of an active, meaning-based approach to the teaching and learning of mathematics. It is hoped that this book will give teachers the information and support they need to create a positive and effective learning environment for their children.

Creating the Learning Environment

2

Part One:
Creating the Learning Environment

The learning environment includes not only the physical layout of the room but also the settings in which children work, the kinds of tasks in which they are engaged, and the way teachers work with their children. All these factors must be considered as we work to create a supportive learning environment.

The learning environment we are aiming for is one that

- Encourages thoughtfulness

- Engages children's thinking

- Provokes questions

- Stimulates a search for meaning

- Encourages children to look for connections and relationships

- Helps children make sense of and understand the mathematics in which they are engaged.

This kind of environment is both realistic and attainable. We can create this kind of classroom, but it does not happen instantly. This learning environment develops over time and is influenced by all the decisions we make, large and small. In this book, we will take a look at the decisions teachers must make and their significance in establishing the desired environment in our classrooms. We must give careful consideration to the way we set up our classroom, the way we present activities to the children, the structures we put in place to support learning, and our interactions with the children.

Our goal

is to create an environment for learning mathematics in which the tasks engage the thinking of each child; the children are expected to work hard and to make responsible choices; we see a high level of commitment, persistence, and independence in each child; and all children have the opportunity to maximize their learning.

3

To create this environment, we may need to give up some of the ways we have managed our classrooms in the past and judge our success in ways that might be new to some of us. We will find that the quiet classroom is not always the most productive classroom, but neither is a classroom that has activity for the sake of activity. Some of you will find it challenging to allow noise and movement as children work. Others will feel anxious when asked to have children experience the same set of tasks over time when that means using fewer of all those "good ideas" we are so eager to share with our children.

If the approach to teaching and learning presented here is new to you, you are bound to encounter some problems and frustrations. We know when we work with children that things will not always go smoothly. It is not necessary that everything go exactly as anticipated. What **is** necessary is a willingness to try and a willingness to be thoughtful and reflective about both things that go well and things that don't. I am confident that if you put these ideas into practice, you will find math time one of the most rewarding times of the day.

How Do We Get Our Classrooms Ready?

One of the first steps to take when creating an environment for learning mathematics is to make sure you have a variety of manipulatives available for the children to work with. To understand the mathematics they are working with, children need to be actively involved with materials.

Materials allow mathematical ideas and
relationships to be modeled. They provide children
with tools for thinking and for testing their ideas.
We must remember, however, that we don't teach
Unifix cubes or pattern blocks or tiles. Rather, we
use them to support children's development of
particular mathematical concepts.

Gather a Variety of Materials

It is important to provide children with several different kinds of manipulatives so they won't associate an idea with a particular material. There is no closed or "best" set of materials, but the following is a list that has proved to be more than satisfactory. It is not necessary to have everything on the list in order to get started. However, if you do have the following materials available, you will be able to provide a rich mathematics program for your students.

Unifix cubes (1000-2000)

Tiles (800)

It is better

to have lots of a few materials than a little of many different materials. Children are more creative when they aren't afraid they will run out of materials.

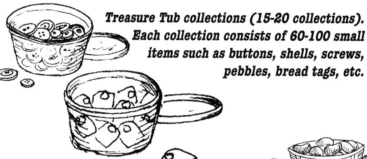

Treasure Tub collections (15-20 collections). Each collection consists of 60-100 small items such as buttons, shells, screws, pebbles, bread tags, etc.

Beans and portion cups (500)

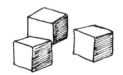

Wooden cubes (400-800)

Toothpicks (not round; 3 or 4 boxes)

Pattern blocks (3 sets)

Geoboards/Geobands (16)

Individual chalkboards and erasers

Containers (various items such as boxes, lids, small food containers, etc.)

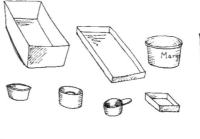

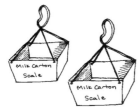

Scales and objects to weigh, such as rocks, apples, oranges, potatoes, clay, small cans of food, balls, small containers of things (such as beans, rice, popcorn, or sand)

Rice and jars: 1 or 2 tubs of rice (or other pourable material such as bird seed or millet); jars of various sizes and shapes, labeled with A, B, C, etc. Various scoops and funnels.

These basic materials will be used for many activities. They should be stored in a place where children have access to them so they can help deliver them to the appropriate places in the room and put them away at the end of the work time.

If built-in

shelving is not available, you can make your own shelves using large concrete bricks and 12-inch-deep boards.

No matter what math program you will be using, when you present various math concepts to children, you will need a variety of supplemental materials such as task cards, recording sheets, and game boards. These can be stored according to the concept they will be used to develop and made available for the children to use when needed.

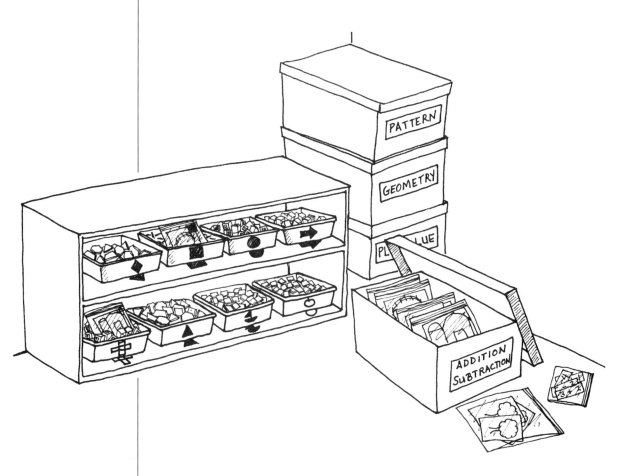

Arrange the Room to Allow for Active Learning

You will need to set up the classroom to accommodate a variety of ways for the children to be actively involved. There are three basic settings that you will need to provide for: the whole class working together, independent stations, and teacher-directed small group work.

When I am setting up a classroom, the first thing I try to create is a large area where the whole class can meet on the floor.

The class needs a place to gather on the rug for whole group instruction.

There are several reasons why this is important. First of all, young children need to be close to the teacher to feel they are a part of the discussion. It is harder for some children to focus on what is happening if the teacher seems far away. (This meeting place also works well for story time, whole group language lessons, and music and movement activities.) A second reason for creating a large floor space is so the whole class can work together with materials on the floor. When everyone is working on the floor, the children can see each other's work. Working on the floor naturally lets children work with each other and gives them some flexibility in using space. Also, when children are sitting in the large group area, the tables and small floor areas are free so that independent activities can be set up around the room. The children can then easily move from the meeting place on the rug to choose where they want to work.

When

arranging my room, I work hard to maximum the space for meeting or working on the floor. We often have too much furniture and need to consider giving some away!

In the past, I have had to set up classrooms where I had 33 children with 33 desks plus extra tables, so I know this can be a challenge. What helped me the most in setting up classrooms was finally realizing I could get rid of some of the furniture. As a teacher who had to work hard over the years to get the furniture I needed, it was difficult to give up the furniture I had, but it certainly made it easier to set up my room once I decided it was all right to do that.

After I have established a large meeting area, I arrange the furniture to create the independent work areas.

I like to *be able to glance around the room and see everybody: no hiding places.*

The desks and/or tables that the children use when doing work in the other subject areas can double as math stations.

I make the whole room available for all projects. Math materials are stored in one place, writing materials and science materials are stored in other places, but the children work anywhere in the room.

Children need table or floor space to work with materials.

Tables work nicely, but if tables are not available, then desks can be pushed together to create "table top" surfaces. Pushing the desks together also helps create room for that large group meeting place. One way that I was able to accommodate many children was to use a piece of plywood as a table. I set the table top on large kindergarten blocks and the children sat on the floor to work. Up to 10 children could sit around this table, and I didn't have to worry about chairs taking up space.

It has worked best for me to have the tables (or clustered desks) serve as work areas for all of the children rather than as personal spaces. The children did not have assigned places at the tables or desks and stored their personal things in "cubbies."

The advantage of this was that children moved from place to place in the room without a sense of being in other people's desks.

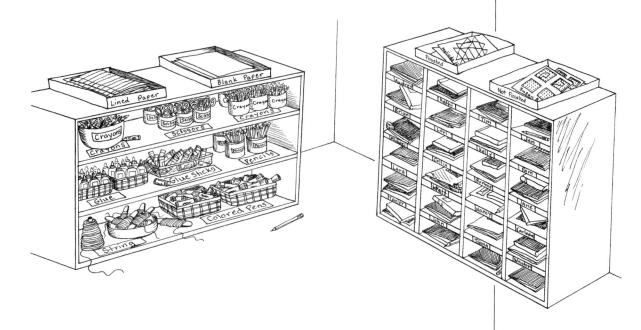

We shared pencils, scissors, crayons, glue, and other supplies, which were stored on a supply shelf. The children had a work folder to store their work in. I also used a Finished Work box and an Not Finished Work box.

Not all teachers choose to set up their rooms the way I did. Some prefer to have children work at their assigned desks during other times of the day, but use the children's desks as math stations during math time.

I didn't need to set up a special place for working with a small group, as I could work with a small group either in the large group rug area or at one of the tables.

When you work with a small group, make sure you are facing the rest of the class so you can easily keep track of what is happening.

The key to setting up your room is to make use of every bit of space.

Pages 14 and 15 show some examples of how teachers have set up their rooms. These classrooms are not large, but the teachers have found ways to accommodate all the various classroom activities.

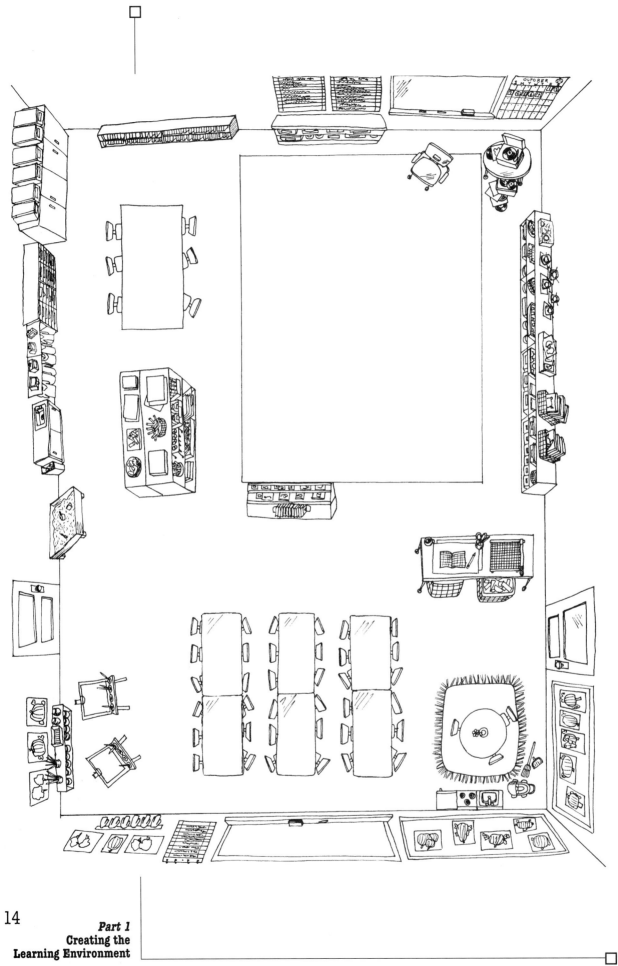

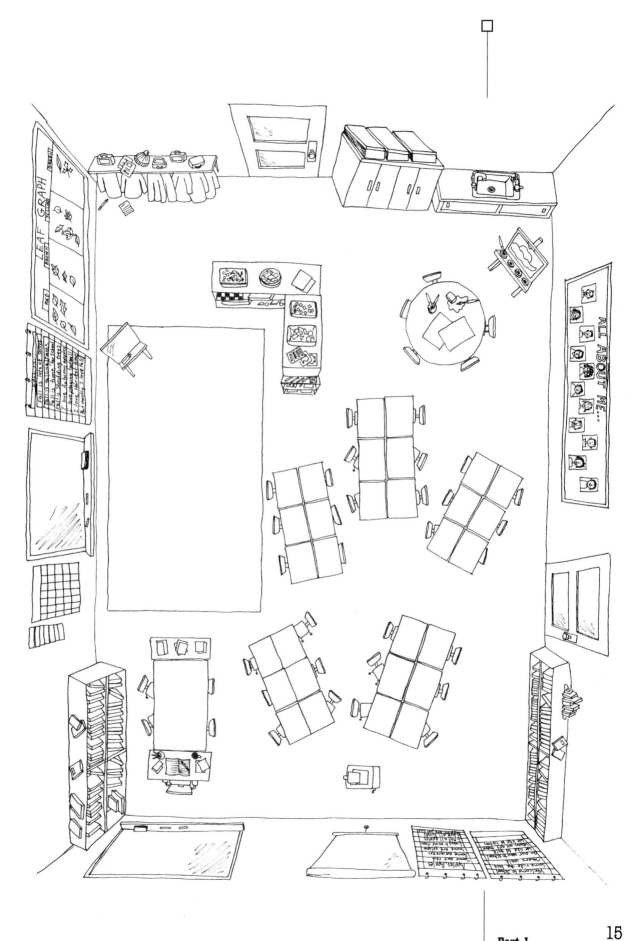

How Do We Help the Children Learn to Work Independently?

If you are going to use materials to teach mathematics, then you must begin every year with a period of several weeks when children are allowed to work with the math materials using their own ideas. We refer to this time as self-directed exploration.

Begin with Self-Directed Exploration

Before children can focus on particular tasks the teacher has in mind for them, they must be given the opportunity to explore materials in their own way. Teachers everywhere have learned for themselves how important this time is. While it may look like play time to those who do not know the purpose or benefits of self-directed exploration, this can be one of the most valuable parts of the math program.

Expect good work. This is not play time.

There is much for the children to learn. Not only do they become familiar with the various materials, but they explore mathematical ideas and learn what the expectations of the classroom are. This time is critical to establishing the learning environment and affects what happens the rest of the year.

Make Note of the Mathematical Ideas that Children Explore and Discover

When we watch children working during self-directed exploration, we will see examples of their creativity and problem-solving abilities. But beyond that, we need to look for the evidence of the mathematics that is naturally occurring. As children become familiar with the attributes and possibilities of the materials, they will naturally

- Create pictures and designs

- Sort in a variety of ways

- Measure

- Build increasingly complex structures

- Encounter problems of balance and symmetry

- Create and extend patterns

- Count and compare quantities

- Use phrases like "longer," "shorter," "not as much as," "more than," "just the same as"

There is a certain amount of trust required from the teacher in order to feel confident that the children are learning in this kind of a setting. Somehow we know when we give children blank paper and pencils or paints that the creative writing or paintings that they produce are more valuable to the child than following someone else's ideas would be. We would not be as impressed with a "fill in the blanks" or "paint by numbers" product. We respect winners at the high school or college level who participate in problem-solving contests that require them to do such things as build models of bridges or other kinds of structures. Young children deserve the same kind of respect for the work they do with materials. By working in this way, children discover the potential of the materials and the power of their own ideas.

Help Children Develop a Work Ethic and Sense of Responsibility

Self-directed exploration time is important not just because of the mathematics to be learned, but also because it provides a wonderful opportunity for children to become familiar with the culture and expectations of the classroom. During this time they will be learning the importance of

- Self-direction and self-discipline

- Decision making

- Choosing tasks and staying with them

- Working independently

- Working hard, staying engaged (without the teacher's attention)

- Working with others — sharing materials and space

- Setting up and putting away

- Inventing, creating, and problem-solving

Establish the Following Procedures

To create this working climate, you must take certain steps and establish certain procedures.

- ***Start with just a few materials.***
  Introduce two or three different materials the first day and then present the rest of them gradually over a period of several days.

- ***Let the children know your expectations for working with the materials.***
  It is very natural for children to work creatively with materials. They know what to do even without direction from the teacher. However, the tone you set will have a big influence on the attitude with which they come to the task. Emphasize the importance of working hard. Since I don't want to imply that this is play time or a time for children to do anything they want, I often use the phrase, "working hard using your own ideas," rather than saying, "You can do what you want with the materials."

There are a few rules that the children need to understand if this time is to go smoothly. The rules for using the materials need to make sense to the children. They need to see that the rules help everyone get along better with each other. I share the following basic rules with the children.

- We do not throw things in the classroom. (Our classroom needs to be a safe place.)

- We share the materials. (We don't need to hoard. We take only what we need as we need it.)

- We clean up before moving to a new station. (This leaves the station ready for the other children so they can have a turn using the materials.)

- We mess up our own work only. (When people create something, they usually want to take it apart themselves. When someone else messes up our work, it feels like they are wrecking it.)

- ***Have the kids set up.***
  We want children to take as much responsibility as possible for their work and actions. One of the ways we encourage this is by giving children responsibility for putting out the materials at the math stations.

  If you set the room up so that certain materials are assigned to certain areas, it is easier for children to deliver them. This also creates a sense of order and predictability in the classroom. When children know where particular materials are going to be, they don't need to wander around checking things out before they make a choice.

Some teachers find it helpful to refer to certain places as the triangle area, the oval area, the arrow station, etc. and then label both the areas and the containers of materials. The children can then easily find where to put the things they are delivering.

When it is time to set up the math stations, have several students put them out at the designated places while you continue an activity (such as rhythmic clapping or counting) with the rest of the children. Some teachers have a group of three or four children assigned as helpers for the week. Other teachers have certain children be helpers on Mondays, a different group on Tuesdays, etc. Still other teachers choose children as they need them. They select children depending on who has been working hard or who needs the opportunity to help.

- **Let the children choose where to work.**
  After the student helpers have set up the materials, dismiss a few children at a time to choose the materials they want to work with. (There should be enough places to work so that even the last child still has a choice.) Allowing the children to make choices is critical in establishing the environment we wish to create. When children choose where they work, they are more interested, involved, and committed than when they feel they are just doing what the teacher asked them to do. Because they are working where they chose to work, we can expect them to be interested and to work hard.

- **Allow the children to choose to work alone or with others.**
  Children generally decide for themselves whether to work alone or with others. Allow children to work together if they are able to make good use of their time. I do not assign children to work together, because the problems that can arise when two children want to do two different things are often beyond their capacity to solve fairly. It is rare that a child always wants to work alone. They usually will move naturally from one mode of working to another.

- **Expect the children to be accountable for working hard.**
  Because one of our goals is helping children learn to make responsible choices, certain parameters should be observed. The children need to understand that making choices is not a license to do anything or choose anything. They need to know the range of the choices: in this case, the choices are the math materials, not Legos or Tinker Toys. There may be another time in the day when all the materials in the room are available to the children, but not

during math time. One reason for this is that our long-range goal is for the children to be ready to do specific activities with the math materials. We want them to be familiar with these particular materials so we can use them for concept development.

It may seem more efficient to assign children to the materials so they will become familiar with all of them. However, asking children to be creative with a material they are not yet interested in proves counterproductive in the long run, and does not move us forward in developing the independence that will prepare them for later independent work. Teachers have found that children will naturally explore all the materials over time. Children who are interested in a material find all kinds of ways to explore it, and other children then become intrigued. One way to ensure a material that has not yet been discovered gets noticed is for you to work with it. Many of the children will love to work side by side with you. There may also be times when you ask the whole class or a small group to work with and discuss a particular material. But that is a distinct experience from this work time, in which choice is essential.

- ***Allow the children to move from place to place whenever they are ready to work with something else.***
  Children's levels of interest and ways of working vary. Some children will choose the same material for several days in a row; others will want to work a little with many different materials before they can really get engaged with any particular one. It usually takes a few days for all of the children to get totally involved — but it does happen.

If you have one or two children who can't seem to get involved, you will need to intervene. There are several different things that you can do to help these children. Some may be overwhelmed with the number of choices. Give them two or three things to choose from. Others may feel they don't know how to do it "right." Sit down and work with these children for a time. If they are having trouble getting started, you might make a simple structure and ask them if they want to copy it. Then have them make something for you to copy. Help them see there is no right or wrong way for them to work with the materials.

It is usually necessary to limit the number of students allowed to work at each station, so children will not run out of materials or space. I usually limit the station to six children at a time. Sometimes the number of chairs around a table will indicate six places. When there are no chairs, the children count to see if there is room for them to work at a particular station.

- **Teach the children a signal to respond to when you need their attention.**
  Whenever you have noise and activity, you need a way to get the children's attention. You will probably want to teach the children to respond to some kind of signal. Ringing a "magic" bell is one way to get children's attention. Or you may want to quietly give a direction such as "hands on your shoulders" or "touch your nose." Children catch on quickly once they see others responding. One of my favorites is an echoing response. The teacher claps a rhythm (clap, clap-clap, clap, clap) and the children respond by clapping the same rhythmic pattern.

- **Tell the children they don't need to come and get you.**
  One of the major goals for self-directed exploration is for children to develop the ability to work independently. This will allow you to work with individual children and small groups as needed. In addition, we want the children to learn not merely to perform for you, but to be engaged

learners in tasks that absorb their attention. (This attitude is actually very important for the children's future. Think about those employers who advertise for "self-starters.")

You want the children to know you are interested in what they are doing, but not to the point that they seek out your attention all the time. Children need to learn that it isn't necessary for you to notice and comment on everything they do. I recommend that you not make yourself available to them whenever they want you. Instead, tell the children that you will come by and see what they're doing when you are ready to do that. If they come to get you, reassure them that you will be coming to see everyone's work in a few minutes. Soon they will trust that you will come by even if they haven't asked you to come and see their work. Your attention will become less and less important to them as they become more and more focused on their work and the sense of accomplishment it brings them.

Give the children plenty of time to work

It is important that you allow at least 45-50 minutes for this "math work time." You will get a higher level of involvement from the children if they don't feel it will be time to clean up before they really get started. If you teach kindergarten for a half-day, you may feel you do not have enough time in your day to devote this much time to mathematics. Some kindergarten teachers have found it is better to have math for longer periods of time three days a week than for a short period of time daily. If possible, arrange your schedule for some flexibility. When children are really engaged you can allow them more time. If they are having trouble focusing on the tasks, be ready to clean up early. However, be patient. There is often a period of restlessness right before a renewed level of involvement. If you feel your children are not being very creative, don't give up too soon. Join in with them and enjoy the materials yourself. It may take several weeks before children really discover the endless possibilities of the materials and their own abilities to create.

Watch closely.

Value their work and creativity.

Get to know your children

At first you may not know what you should be doing when the children are busy with their own ideas. Your most important job is to stand back and observe. This is a wonderful time for you to learn about your children, and the information you get will help you immensely in making decisions about your children and their needs.

Watch to see how they work. Do they work alone or with others? How do they respond if another child accidentally bumps their work? Do they stay focused on one material, or do they move from material to material? Do they share easily, or do they need to be reminded? Do they like to talk about what they are doing, or do they work without talking? Are their creations simple or complex? Do they like to organize or build with symmetry, or are they more random in their approach? Do they make designs or structures, or do they think of what they build as houses or castles or robots?

You may want to take notes on what you observe about your children. Some children are actually motivated by seeing that their work is important enough for you to write down.

Your presence and interest in their work will help communicate to the children that what they are doing is important. However, because we want children to work for the satisfaction of their own learning and not just to please the teacher, do not judge or comment on their work other than to say something like "It looks like you've been working hard" or "Was that fun to do?" or "Tell me about what you are working on."

Follow the children's lead when interacting with them

Resist the urge to become over-involved in the children's work. When you do engage a child in a discussion, try to elicit talk from them about what they are doing, rather than just imposing your thoughts on them. Sometimes simply asking, "Tell me about what you made (or are working on)," will be sufficient and the child will either respond eagerly with some detail or very briefly, getting right back to work. When the child is at a point in the work that he or she wants to talk about it, finding the words to tell you what he or she has done or has made can be beneficial and also can provide an opportunity for you to model the use of certain words in the context of what the child is doing. For example, if a child says, "I like these tiles. They are really shiny and soft," you could comment, "I don't think these tiles are soft like a teddy bear, but they are really smoo-o-oth. When I feel them, there are no bumps. Is that what you were noticing?"

Sometimes our questions interrupt rather than enhance or support the children's work. I had a friend who once said, "I drop questions on my kids. Some of them stick and some of them slide off." I think this is a good attitude with which to approach your interactions when the children are working. Sometimes you will stimulate an new idea or exploration by asking a question; other times you won't. Examples of open-ended questions you can ask are:

"What do you think would happen if . . . ?"
"How many do you think it would take to . . . ?"
"Do you have another idea . . . ?"

Intervene if necessary

Because this is such a natural way for children to work, you will find most children actively engaged during this time. Discipline problems occur less often than they might in other situations. While the children should be allowed to work with minimum interruptions, they should not be allowed to be unproductive or disruptive to others. The children who are not handling this period of time well will stand out, and you can intervene as necessary. If children sometimes wander or fail to become engaged, ask them to tell you where they are planning to work. You may need to walk with them to the place where they will work, check on them in a few minutes to see how they are doing, and in some cases take away the privilege of moving freely from station to station. Any children who choose to work together but distract each other and do not get to work may have to have the privilege of working together taken away for a period of time. Later you can provide opportunities for them to try again to work productively together.

Teachers who imagined self-directed exploration as a version of playground activity will be pleasantly surprised at the hard work and productivity that most of the children will display. As long as the children know this is not play time and know what the expectations are, you can expect this to be a busy and active but rewarding time for everyone.

Establish guidelines for clean-up time

The children should be responsible for clean-up time and for putting materials back where they belong. For this to go smoothly, it is necessary to have some guidelines. Children need to know that they are to clean up their own creations and that it is not helpful to have someone else come and take apart what you have worked hard to create.

The children need to know where to put the materials and where they are to go after they have cleaned up their work area.

It helps to have something interesting going on, such as a song, rhythmic pattern, or finger play so they will be motivated to clean up quickly and go to their places on the rug. Sometimes two or three "housekeepers" can go around and make sure all the pieces are picked up and all the tubs and baggies of material are back where they belong.

Discuss How Things Went

At the end of the math period, it is very important that you gather the children together to discuss how things went. This should usually be a very brief time, but it is vitally important. This is another opportunity for you to let the children know that you value qualities like hard work, sharing, getting along, and using their own ideas. You can tell them what you noticed that showed you they were using this time well. A few children can share what they did and/or how they worked. Even though just a few children share each day, this sharing validates the importance of the work time to all the children.

If there happens to be a problem on a particular day with noise or too much wandering or silliness, the children will usually be able to identify the problem and discuss what needs to happen in the future. When things go well, they will be able to recognize that as well.

Resist allowing this time to become a sharing time for everyone. It is difficult for children to listen to each other for long periods, and this is not the best use of math time. It is more meaningful for young children to talk about their work while they are actually working. The children should have many other opportunities to talk about their work and to learn to express themselves as they interact with others or with you during their work time.

First grade teacher Kathy McGrath adapted the idea of "working levels" to meet the needs of her first graders. A few weeks after school starts, when the children have had enough experiences to be able to be reflective about the math period, she introduces them to Working Levels. Working Levels are designed to help raise the children's awareness of their behavior, to make the expectations more explicit, and to give focus to discussions about what it means to work hard.

There are five working levels that the children become familiar with:

Level 0	Level 1	Level 2	Level 3	Level 4
Bothers others	Not working	Works when reminded	Responsible Respectful	Responsible Respectful Helps Others

If you decide to use the working levels, you will find that the discussions that are generated are more important than the levels themselves as children learn what it means to work hard. Be specific and concrete with the children as you discuss such questions as "What does it look like to work hard?" "What does it look like to be responsible?" "How can we be helpful to others?" "What kinds of things would not be helpful?" "What will we see? What will we hear?"

Together with the children, you will identify such things as "Working hard means staying with a job and not wandering around." "It means concentrating on what you are doing and not just talking." "It is not helping others if you mess up their work or do their work for them." "It may be helping others if you help them pick up materials they spilled, but you need to ask first and make sure it is all right to do that."

The children should decide for themselves how they think they did and share their feelings about their work only if they want to. Young children are usually quite honest and are willing to acknowledge if they had difficulty settling down to work on a particular day or if they feel they worked especially hard.

The levels are not intended to be used to label the children themselves but to give them a way of thinking about how that particular day went and to help them become more aware of their behavior. This is not intended to put pressure on children to be perfect, but to help them be honestly reflective.

How Long Should the Children Explore?

Give the children opportunities to work independently with the materials several times a week for several weeks. (Kindergarten children will need at least 12 weeks, first grade children will need six to eight weeks, and second grade children will need four to six weeks.) The level of involvement and the complexity of the children's work evolves over time. The tone and expectations you set during self-directed time will establish the classroom environment for the other activities you plan to do for the rest of the year.

Don't rush through this. It is important to establish a productive work environment. What you do now will affect the whole year!

How Do We Know When to Move On?

Although you may be anxious to move on to the more structured work with concept development, if you leave exploration too soon, you will not get all the benefits from it. It is important to stay with this long enough to see that the children have learned to work hard and to work independently.

Sometimes teachers attempt to move the children too fast to concept development activities. When that happens, the children let us know. They lack the focus and the enthusiasm for the work that we might expect. Even very experienced teachers have to be reminded of this on occasion. A friend of mine taught a first and second grade multi-age class for the first time after years of teaching first grade. After three weeks of self-directed exploration, she was feeling the need to begin pattern activities with her second grade students sooner than she would have moved her first graders in the past. She worried that the second graders were ready for more of a challenge and she didn't want to hold any of them back. What she found was that the children had difficulty focusing on the tasks they had been assigned. They didn't seem deliberately resistant, but they didn't get much accomplished. She picked up on these

I feel more
relaxed about the
time allotted to self-
directed exploration
if, at the same time,
I begin concept
development work
through whole group
teacher-directed
activities for five to
15 minutes a day.

clues and gave the children two more weeks of exploration time. This was time well spent, as it was followed by an exciting period when the children worked eagerly with increasing patterns and patterns on the 00-99 chart.

If you find out the hard way that you have moved the children to structured activities too soon, go back to self-directed exploration for a time. Then, when you reintroduce the structured activities, you will see the difference!

How Do We Transition from Exploration to Concept Development?

When children have shown that they can work independently in pursuing their own ideas, you can begin making the transition to structured activities by providing opportunities for directed exploration at some of the stations. For example, you could put out recording materials with the pattern blocks or geoboards so the children can make records of their designs. You will get an idea of which children are ready for more structure by the level of interest at these stations.

When you have some stations where children are allowed to use their own ideas and other stations where they have a specific task to do, make sure the children understand the difference between them. It is not appropriate for you to allow them to work freely at a station if it is set up for a specific task. You want them to understand that sometimes there is particular work that you expect them to do.

You can have both free exploration and structured tasks going on at the same time if it is clear when they can choose what they do with a material and when the material is there for a specific task. For example, the pattern blocks on the floor may still be available for exploration while the pattern blocks that are on the table along with a tub of recording materials are used to make records.

Gradually replace all of the self-directed exploration stations with specific tasks by introducing a few tasks at a time until all of the stations are concept development activities. You can put the materials you need for a particular station in a tub or baggie and have the children set up the stations. Establish particular places for the stations to be delivered. This helps the children know what the choices are and keeps them from wandering around the room trying to decide where to work.

Periodically throughout the year, give the children some time to work again with the materials using their own ideas. During this time, you will often see evidence that they are applying the concept development work they have been doing. Some teachers also allow the children to work with the math materials when they have free time during the day. That way, exploration can continue concurrently with concept development.

Concept Development

PART 2

What Concepts Should We Be Teaching?

What Kinds of Tasks Support the
Development of Concepts?

How Can We Meet the Range of
Needs in Our Classroom?

Do We Need a Separate Math Time?

What Needs to be Considered
When We Integrate Math into
Other Curriculum Areas?

The time we spend creating the learning environment is critically important because once we have this learning environment established, we can present experiences to children in ways that maximize children's developing understanding of mathematical concepts. Children need multiple experiences with a set of related activities that give them the opportunity to gain a broad and complete understanding of whatever concept(s) we want them to learn. And they need lots of time to work with these concepts so they can develop understanding and facility. Children will not have the opportunity to develop a deep understanding of math concepts if they are given a random collection of experiences in which no concept is fully developed and their individual needs are not considered.

When we begin our work with concept development, our first job is to determine what mathematical concepts our children need to know and understand.

What Concepts Should We Be Teaching?

The standards set by the National Council of Teachers of Mathematics indicate that children need experiences beyond the arithmetic traditionally taught in schools. In addition to their work with number, it is recommended that children study patterns and relationships, measurement, geometry, and probability and statistics. While I agree that it is important that we provide a range of mathematical experiences beyond number, I think we must keep the development of number concepts at the heart of the mathematics program for young children.

Children
need multiple experiences with a set of related activities.

41

We should not underestimate the importance of building a strong foundation in number. What children know and understand about number impacts their work with all other mathematical topics. The study of number concepts cannot be squeezed in as just one of many topics that children work with. Children need ongoing and multiple opportunities to develop number sense: to count and compare quantities, to add and subtract, and to work with place value in ways that ask them to think and reason, to see relationships and to make connections.

What

children know and understand about number impacts their work with all other mathematical topics.

As we seek to broaden the children's mathematical experiences beyond number, we must make sure the concepts and ideas we present are meaningful to them. Too often we try to present concepts and ideas before children can make sense of them. We cannot assume that recommendations for teaching particular concepts to older children are necessarily appropriate for younger children.

We will not prepare children to work with mathematical concepts that they cannot understand by simplifying tasks just so they can learn to do them at an earlier age and can appear to be working with advanced mathematical ideas. What we need to do instead is give them experiences that build the proper foundation so that they will be appropriately prepared for whatever mathematics they encounter in the future. For example, fourth or fifth grade children who are studying patterns and functions could be asked to solve a problem referred to as the Handshake Problem: "Our class has 28 children. If everyone in the class shook hands with everyone else, how many handshakes would there be?" The children could solve the problem by making the problem simpler, acting it out, and looking for a pattern.

It might seem reasonable for first grade teachers to prepare their children for this problem by giving them a simpler version of it, such as: "If the three bears all gave each other a hug, how many hugs would there be?" While the problem appears to be a simpler version of the handshake problem, the kind of thinking required by the children has little or nothing to do with the kind of thinking required to do the handshake problem.

Children would be better served if they worked on developing the concept of patterns through a wide variety of experiences so they could bring an understanding of pattern to the task when it is presented in all its complexity at the appropriate time. Our work in primary grades is to build a strong foundation that helps children make sense of their work with mathematics.

What Kinds of Tasks Support the Development of Concepts?

Teachers who become enthusiastic about activity-based learning often begin a search for unique and exciting activities. They prepare elaborate experiences, thinking that is the key to the children's interest and growth in mathematics. However, the most important thing about a task is that it require the children to think. Tasks do not have to be complicated to engage children in thinking. When we understand and respect the complexity of the seemingly simple work young children do, we will see that what may seem simple to us is not really simple at all. In fact, it is often the tasks that appear to be simplest that lead to the most focused attention on the mathematics involved.

To be most effective, the tasks must make sense to the children and be simple enough so that learning the directions doesn't get in the way. We want the children to focus on understanding the concepts and not get lost in the directions for doing the task.

The most powerful tasks have value in being repeated over and over again. Each time children do a task they will be working at a different level as they develop understanding and increase competence.

Our work in primary grades is to build a strong foundation that helps children make sense of their work with mathematics.

When we understand and respect the complexity of the seemingly simple work young children do, we will see that what may seem simple to us is not really simple at all.

Consider the following activity: "How many different seven-sided figures can you make on the geoboard?"

The directions for doing this task are easily understood by children, so in that sense it is a simple task. However, actually doing the task can be quite challenging and complex. If we watch children at work, we will see their surprise when they think they have added a side only to find out they have ended up with the same number they started with or that they added two sides instead of one. When children first work with this task, they count and recount to check the number of sides. Then, with experience, they begin to be more deliberate and eventually develop strategies for adding or taking away sides. This increasing competence can develop only if they have many different opportunities to work with this task.

Measuring yarn using paper clips and Unifix cubes as the units of measure is another simple task that requires complex thinking on the part of the child. While measuring the yarn, the children can

- estimate ("I think it will take 23 paper clips.")

- check and revise their estimates ("I've already used 15 paper clips and there's lots of yarn left to measure. I'm changing my mind. Now I think it will take 35 paper clips.")

- organize into tens and ones ("Every time I get to 10 paper clips, I mark it by putting another paper clip next to it. Then I can tell how many I have without counting each one.")

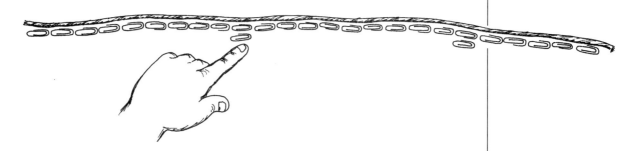

- record numerals ("I counted 32 paper clips. I can write that number down.")

- see relationships ("I used 32 paper clips. The Unifix cubes are smaller. I think it will take about 40 Unifix cubes.")

- compare ("It took 32 paper clips and 59 Unifix cubes. It took 27 more Unifix cubes than paper clips.")

There are many advantages to using simple tasks with children. We will not spend a lot of time preparing or organizing material or teaching children complicated procedures. We will then be able to focus on the interactions that are such an important part of the teaching and learning process.

How Can We Meet the Range of Needs in Our Classroom?

Meeting all the individual needs in our classroom is a big challenge. However, if we are careful about the tasks we choose, we can reach this goal. Rather than presenting different tasks to different children, a more manageable approach is to provide tasks that are "expandable" and thus fit the needs of various children depending on how they approach the task.

Our goal should be for all of our children to work to what I call the "edge of their understanding." That means they all need to be working with tasks that are appropriately challenging for them, no matter what their abilities or experiences. Children should not be doing tasks that are out of reach and have no meaning for them, but there should also be no upper limit to what the children can learn, notice, discover, question, or wonder about the tasks they are doing.

The following is an example of how one task might meet a range of needs depending on how each child approaches the task.

Instead of measuring the length of a piece of yarn, a group of second graders made various shapes using pieces of yarn. Their job was to figure out how many tiles fit in the shapes.

The children were focused on different skills as they worked with the task.

Some children were getting practice counting.

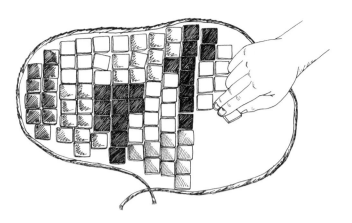

Other children were beginning to develop strategies for organizing to make counting easier and using color to form groups of ten.

One child was finding a shortcut and filling one-half of the shape and doubling the number instead of counting each tile.

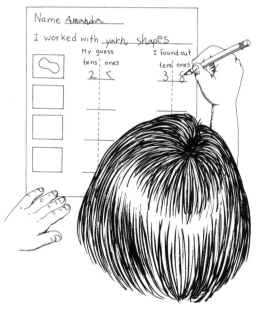

Other children were comparing their estimates to the actual count and figuring out the difference.

While the children were generally focused on number concepts when they worked with the yarn shapes, the task also provided them an opportunity to look informally at the relationships between area and perimeter. Jolene figured out that she can make a shape that uses a very small number of tiles if she makes it long and skinny.

Mikkal wanted to make the biggest shape he could and formed a circle.

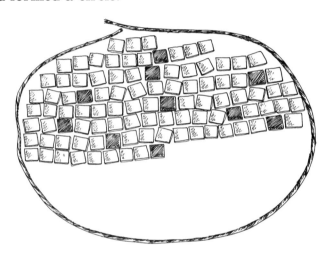

Each child is getting something different from the task, but every child is learning and every child is challenged.

We can most effectively meet the range of needs in our class if we allow children the opportunity to work on problems using their own methods and approaches. To a large extent, when tasks are expandable, children will naturally work at an appropriate level. However, we must also be alert to opportunities to help children gain the most benefit from the tasks. We need to watch and listen as they work, interacting with them and offering support and challenges when needed.

Do We Need a Separate Math Time?

As we begin to see that mathematics is more than arithmetic, we begin to see mathematics all around us and come to appreciate it as a tool for exploring and making sense of the world. We see opportunities for mathematics to be a part of the study of many topics. We see how mathematics helps us understand, organize, and analyze our experiences in science. We see the connection between mathematics and music as we explore rhythm and patterns. We see the relationships between mathematics and art as we work with symmetry and design. We see the mathematics in the structures children create. We find that gathering and organizing data helps us solve problems and understand many different situations.

Because mathematics can be a part of so many different subject areas, some have concluded that a separate math program is less than desirable. However, not having a separate math time can lead to a lack of focus on particular math concepts. There is a danger that mathematics could become an incidental part of the curriculum, causing children to end up with little depth of understanding. Just because there may be opportunities to learn mathematics while playing in the housekeeping corner or studying lady bugs, it is not an automatic, inevitable, or even likely result.

It is simply not enough to have mathematics come up incidentally. We must be purposeful in planning experiences that will help our students develop specific mathematical understandings. This means we need to set up particular, predictable times to work with mathematics. There needs to be a math time during which the whole class and the teacher are focused on mathematics.

What Needs to be Considered When We Integrate Math into Other Curriculum Areas?

While mathematics can be a natural part of the study of many topics, much of what is called integration through theme-based instruction is not really integration at all. Consider a common practice using a theme of bears. It could be assumed that children are studying about bears in order to learn more about them. But an understanding of bears is not enhanced by estimating the number of gummy bears in a jar, nor by measuring a teddy bear. If the theme is intended to be a study of bears and a context for learning mathematics, then our work with bears should enhance the children's understanding of both bears and mathematics. But what often happens is that the children do not learn either topic well. It's not necessary to have theme-related materials in order to discover relationships and develop a sense of quantity. For example, children can be productively engaged when estimating the number of marbles it takes to fill a jar and then comparing that to the number of pecans it takes. Using gummy bears is irrelevant and only creates the illusion that there is a meaningful context. If there is no natural real-world connection to the topic, it is better not to try to force a connection.

Although using themes to organize and bring meaning to content can be a valuable approach to learning many important concepts and ideas, we must be very thoughtful when applying this idea to our study of mathematics. One of the problems with giving children mathematical experiences when working with a theme is that they usually do any particular task only once. One measuring experience will not help children develop an understanding of measurement. Children need to be immersed in the concept of measuring if they are to deepen their understanding. If we choose math tasks because they go with a theme rather than because we want to support the development of a particular mathematical idea, we will not be providing the in-depth work our children need.

It's not necessary to have theme-related materials in order to discover relationships and develop a sense of quantity.

If we choose math tasks because they go with a theme rather than because we want to support the development of a particular mathematical idea, we will not be providing the in-depth work our children need.

We want children to understand and make sense of the mathematics they are learning. This means that the situations in which children work must make sense to them, but it does not mean that these situations must be "real life" applications. Sorting a box of buttons and looking for patterns on the 1-100 chart can be important mathematical experiences for children. There is richness, power, and beauty in the study of mathematics itself that those of us who experienced mathematics as memorized procedures did not enjoy.

Appropriate Settings for Learning

Part Three:
Appropriate Settings for Learning

We need to be able to use a variety of settings to support children's learning of math concepts. Some activities are best presented in a whole group, teacher-directed setting; other activities should be presented as independent work; and some activities should be presented by the teacher to small groups of children.

How Do We Decide Which Setting to Use?

Each of these settings serves different purposes and provides different opportunities for the children. I think of the various settings as options I can use depending on what I think will allow me to make the best use of our time.

Working with the whole class at once is the organizational structure that is effective for giving certain kinds of instructions and directions that you don't want to have to repeat over and over again. There are also ongoing activities, such as estimating and opening activities, that can be done effectively with the whole class. The independent work time can be the most effective and most productive setting, as it is the organizational structure that allows us most closely to match children's individual needs, styles, and interests. Working with a small group allows you to really watch, interact with, and respond to individual children during a "teaching" time.

Whole Group Time: What Kinds of Work Should Be Done with the Whole Class?

There are certain activities that are effectively and efficiently done with the whole class. However, we must be careful to make sure during this time that children are continuously thinking and engaged.

Be aware of how you work with the whole group, especially if you find that the whole class is responding as one voice. A group response may be appropriate, but usually it indicates a memorized response that individual children may or may not understand. These kinds of responses may indicate knowledge that may be of value, but they are not responses that require thinking and understanding. One of the biggest problems with whole group work is the assumption we often make that all (or even most) of the children understand what they are saying in chorus. For example, when you ask a group of children, "How many tens?" and "How many ones?" when they are looking at a number like 76, you will most likely get correct responses. It will only be in other settings like independent work time that you will be able to tell if these words have any meaning for them.

The following are the kinds of activities that are appropriate in a whole class setting.

Introduction or Review of Activities (Even the youngest children can learn tasks this way.)

It is an efficient use of time to introduce activities to everyone at once. If there are individual children who don't learn how to do the task when it is introduced to the whole class, the other children will be able to help them. Make sure the children know they should ask another child if they are unsure of the directions, rather than coming to you. That way they will learn to be independent, and you will be able to work with children who really need your help.

Make sure
the children are
thinking and
engaged.

Ongoing Activities

There are certain ongoing activities that work well as whole group activities, such as opening activities, estimating activities, and graphing. However, because children need to be involved in doing their own work as much as possible, keep this time short. Remember to get the children thinking as much as possible rather than simply responding along with the group. For example, all the children can be involved in estimating the number of walnuts it takes to fill a jar. Even though the teacher is the one to fill the jar while the children count the walnuts, there is a sense of active participation as they watch the jar being filled and compare what they thought was going to happen with what actually happens.

Shared Experiences

There are some activities that the whole class can experience at once if there are enough materials for all the children to work with at one time. For the tasks to be appropriate for the whole group, all the children should be able to do the same task, each in their own way. They should not be kept together or directed step by step through the tasks. For example, the children can work with activities such as sorting collections or making increasing patterns with a variety of materials.

Independent Work Time: How Can We Make Sure Independent Work Time is Productive?

The time during which children work independently is very important, as this is when they are fully responsible for the work they are doing and when they get the practice and experiences they need. Most of the time they should be working with tasks they have chosen from a set of related tasks. Occasionally they should also work with tasks assigned by the teacher.

Have Children Choose from Among Related Topics

Whenever you provide children the opportunity to choose where they are going to work, you must make sure that they are getting the experiences they need, no matter which activities they choose. This means you need to provide a set of activities that all deal with the same concept. For example, if the children are working with addition and subtraction, all the choices would give them various ways to practice addition and subtraction.

Establish the Following Procedures

The underlying structure of the independent work time is much like the structure used during self-directed exploration, so similar procedures need to be in place.

- **Introduce the activities to the whole class.** Introduce each activity to the whole class before putting it out at a station where children will be working independently. Introduce the activities over a period of several days, gradually replacing the familiar ones with new ones until eight to 10 tasks dealing with the same concept are available for the children to choose from.

  The way you present the tasks to the children will make a big difference in how they think about them. Since we are trying to establish an attitude of active participation rather than one of passively following directions, introduce the tasks as questions to be answered or problems to be solved rather than tasks to be completed.

  There are very subtle differences in these two approaches to presenting the tasks: one way discourages thinking and the other encourages thinking. For example, a teacher might introduce making geoboard designs by saying, "Your job is to make geoboard designs that have seven sides. Make sure you count the sides carefully and then record them on the paper." Or the teacher could turn it into a question by saying instead, "How many different ways can you make shapes with seven sides? It will help you to keep track of all the ways you find if you make records of each of the ways as you find them." The first way of presenting the task leads the children to focus on getting the task done. With the second way, the children will probably be engaged differently, as they are encouraged to find as many different ways as they can.

Introduce the tasks as problems to be solved rather than tasks to be completed.

Let's consider another example. Measuring the number of scoops that could fit in a jar can also be introduced in two different ways. One way focuses on how to do the task: "Here are the jars. You are to fill each one with scoops of rice and record how many scoops each jar holds." By introducing the task another way, the teacher can involve the children in thinking by asking the children to estimate first: "How many scoops of rice do you think this jar will hold?" After measuring out a few scoops, the teacher could then ask the children to consider the information gathered thus far and make adjustments: "Now that we see that three scoops filled the jar up to here, does anyone want to change their mind about the number of scoops the jar will hold?"

Introducing the task in this way models the thought process the teacher wants the children to use when doing the task on their own. The goal is for the children to continue asking these questions for themselves even when working independently.

When the directions for doing the tasks are simple, they need very little introduction. It is important not to over-introduce the tasks so that they will remain intriguing for the children.

If the directions are somewhat complicated, take a few minutes at the beginning of math time for a period of two or three days to go over the instructions. When most of the children know what to do, put it out at an independent station. Don't worry if there are a few children who do not know exactly how to do the tasks. The other children will be able to help them. Encourage them to help each other rather than to come to you for further directions.

When you have new tasks out, spend a day or two watching how the children work with them so you can redirect them (or reteach the activity to the whole class if necessary).

- ***Have the children set up.***
  If you have the materials for each activity organized in tubs or baggies, you can have the children set up the stations. I generally prepare station materials to accommodate six children at a time. The particular materials needed for the task, such as task cards and recording sheets, are put in baggies or tubs, and other basic materials, such as pattern blocks, toothpicks, or geoboards, can be added to the station by the children.

- **Let the children choose where to work and move from place to place whenever they are ready to work with something else.**

  Our goal is to maintain a high level of involvement. Just as when children were exploring materials, the level of involvement will be greater if the child has made the selection. If you have provided a set of activities that all deal with a particular concept, children can choose the task they want to work with and still be getting the experiences they need. For example, if all of the tasks deal with counting, it doesn't matter which counting task the child works with. Or if all the tasks deal with place value, the child will be getting appropriate experiences no matter which station he or she chooses.

  Choosing where to work does not imply that one can also choose not to work. On the contrary, the expectation is that a child will work harder because he or she has chosen what to work with. Just as was true during self-directed exploration, if a child cannot make a choice and tends to wander, you can offer a narrower range of choices. You might say something like, "Do you want to make creations with the lids or do you want to record pattern block designs?"

- **Make sure the children know they are accountable for working hard.**

  When children are allowed to move from station to station, they need to understand that that does not mean they are allowed to wander or waste time. Since many activities are open-ended and do not have recording sheets to go along with them, it is not obvious when a child has "finished his work." Some children will show evidence of more than you expected, and others will have less to show for their time with the task.

The children will decide for themselves when to move on to another task. What you need to do is check to make sure each child is working hard, regardless of whether they accomplish a lot or a little.

If some children are wandering or wasting time, you can set goals for them and come back to see if they have accomplished the goal. For example, you might say, "I would like to see if you can make a pattern all the way to the edge of the rug. I will come back later and see how you did."

- *Allow children to come back to the same activity as many times as they wish to.*
  One of the advantages of an independent work time that allows children to make choices about where to work is that it provides opportunities for the children to get lots of practice. Children learn from the repetition of the tasks. Some teachers have felt children were more accountable if they kept a record sheet of where they had gone each day. While it may seem like this would help children to be more accountable, what actually happens is that the children begin to focus on getting the tasks done and checking them off rather than getting engaged in the work itself.

  It is not necessary for you or the children to keep track of where they have worked. It is more important to make sure the children are productively engaged and that you see signs of their growth as they work with whatever task they have chosen.

- *Allow children to work alone or with others.*
  Children will naturally work together with other children who have chosen the same tasks. Talking while they work can be an important part of their learning. Even though there often will be tasks designed to be done with partners, I do not recommend assigning partners. I allow the children to find partners when and if they happen to choose a partner game. If a child cannot find a partner, he or she will often just play the partner game alone. Requiring children to work in pairs during a time in which children must decide where to work and how long to work there can create problems that are difficult for children to solve at this age, and this can distract them from the mathematical work they are to be doing.

- *Remind the children that they don't need to come and get you.*
  While you want to be very involved in what the children are doing as they work independently, you also want to foster independence so you can work with individual children and small groups when appropriate. Remind the children that they don't need to come and get you to

show you what they are working on. Encourage them to talk to the other children if a problem arises to see if they can solve it before bringing it to the teacher. If there are persistent problems that children need help solving, then you need to deal with them during a whole class time so all the children know how to cope with the particular situation.

Get to know your children and respond to their needs

Observing the children while they work is one of our most important jobs. Once the stations are introduced and the children know what to do, you can focus on what the children are doing. How the children do the tasks will become as important and as revealing as what they do. As you observe the children, you will be able to see whether any children need more instruction, whether the activities are too hard or too easy, or whether there is a common misunderstanding you need to deal with.

You can also interact with the children, providing support and presenting challenges. If you have parent helpers or assistants in the room, help them learn to observe the children first to see how they work with the task before they intervene. It is important that all the adults in the room know they should intervene only when necessary and then only to help the children work on their own.

Intervene if necessary

Sometimes children say they are bored when they mean they want some adult attention. They may not be used to taking responsibility for themselves. They could be having trouble making a choice, or perhaps some are having difficulty accepting the fact that they didn't get their first choice. Some children just need to be redirected. You may say something like, "I would like you to choose a task and I will come by later to see how you are doing." Once in a while, you may find it helpful to work with a child for a few minutes on a task he or she chooses. You can check to make sure the task is not too hard, and you can help the child see that he or she can get engaged in the task.

Have the stations available for the children to work with for several weeks

One of the keys to this approach, and one of the hardest aspects for many teachers to accept, is the idea that the same activities should be available for children to work with for several weeks. In an environment that supports concept development, children are allowed the time they need to become proficient with these ideas. When new activities are introduced, it takes a few days for children to become deeply involved. The first step for children is just knowing how to do an activity. Expect that the children will become more involved after a few days rather than less involved. It takes a few days to "get into it."

When the tasks are appropriate, you will see the children working hard, making a few mistakes, double-checking to see whether they did it right. After several days or even a few weeks, you will see less intensity as the tasks become easier for them. You will begin to see less concentration and sense a little more restlessness. When you ask questions and they know the answers quickly without having to figure then out, then it is time to move on.

Occasionally present children with assigned tasks

On occasion you will want to assign particular tasks for children to do rather than having them choose. Assigned tasks do not generally meet the range of needs in the same way that providing choices does. However, there may be times when assigning tasks is appropriate. There may be a particular activity or set of activities that everyone needs to experience, so giving them choices does not work. This will be particularly important if each of the tasks focuses on a different topic or strand.

There may also be times when you may want to give children assignments that require a minimum of movement and decision making on the part of the children so you can focus your attention more fully on a small group or individual assessments.

The following is an example of a set of activities that the teacher wants all her children to work with because they give children experiences with different areas of the math curriculum. She has divided her class into four groups and assigned them the following tasks.

At one table, the teacher has asked the children to sort various collections in as many ways as they can.

At the next table, the teacher is giving the children the experiences they need to prepare them for later, more structured work with toothpicks. The children are creating toothpick pictures using their own ideas.

At another table, the children are copying geoboard designs.

At another table children make circles by tracing around lids. They then cut these circles into halves and fourths and make border patterns with these shapes.

Even when I have various stations I want all the children to work with, there are several reasons why I would still not rotate the children through the stations.

From a practical classroom management perspective, when we set up stations for children to rotate through, we create a situation in which we need to find activities that can be fit into a certain time slot rather than activities that meet a certain need.

Children do not work or learn at the same pace nor stay interested and focused for the same amount of time. Some children will invariably feel rushed and others will feel restless and bored.

When children are directed to move from activity to activity at a given signal, the children are not asked to assume the responsibility for learning or even for using their time effectively. Rather, the teacher is in control and the emphasis in on doing the activity in the time allotted rather than on learning a concept, developing a skill, or becoming truly engaged in the task. The motivation becomes external rather than internal, and the teacher's job can become one of keeping the children on task and/or taking care of discipline problems.

Instead of a rotation, I have used what I call a flip flop. I divide the children into four heterogeneous groups and assign each group a task. I want to allow for different finishing times, so I schedule an unstructured time (such as snack time, recess, free reading or working with chalkboards) following the work time. Then, at the beginning of another period (like after recess or even the next day), children will go on to a different task. The key is that children have a place to go when they finish rather than moving to one of the assigned tasks. This allows children who work at different speeds to finish at various times.

Small Group Time: How Can We Work Effectively with Small Groups?

Working with a small group allows you to really watch, interact with, and respond to individual children during a "teaching" time. You can use this instructional time in three ways:

- to introduce activities that are difficult to introduce to the whole group

- to observe more closely and thus to assess the needs of children without having to do individual interviews

- to provide experiences to meet the needs of a particular group of children.

Small group instructional time is particularly important for some children who find it more difficult to be as engaged and focused when they are part of a large group than when they are part of a small group.

Try to be flexible in the use of small group time. Groups do not need to be set up permanently but can be formed when particular needs arise. You can meet for very short periods with some groups and for longer periods with others. You may want to meet with some groups for several days in a row if they need extra help or an extra challenge. Teachers have told me that they don't think it is fair to spend more time with some children than with others. They are concerned that they are always responding to the kids who are struggling and trying to find ways to challenge those children who are way ahead of the others, and they worry about the kids in the middle who are always getting overlooked. I agree that it is important to meet the needs of every child in our class. However, that should not be measured in time spent with the teacher. Rather, our goal should be to find a way for all children to work at the edge of their understanding.

Some groups will need to meet with you briefly every few days and will be able to accomplish

Be flexible.
Some children will need to meet with you more often than others.

much by working independently. Other children will need more teacher guidance to focus on the concepts and will need to meet with you more often.

Prepare the Children for Work with Small Groups

Before you can work effectively with small groups, you will need to prepare the class. The following guidelines will help you teach the children how they are to handle themselves during this time.

- *Make sure the children know how to work independently before you expect them to work without bothering you when you are busy with a small group. Have them practice not interrupting you ahead of time.*
  Before you actually pull out a group, tell the children that you are planning to work with small groups during math time. Let them know it is important that they not interrupt you when you are working with the group. Tell them you are going to watch them that day and see if they can work independently without bothering the teacher. Spend at least one period having them show you how well they can work. If any problems come up, discuss with them how they should be handled if you are busy. The first time you work with a small group, make it a very short period so they can be successful.

- *Make sure the children know all the independent activities before you pull out a small group. Don't pull a group out if you have just introduced new activities.*
  The activities need to be familiar so the children can be expected to know exactly what to do without bothering you.

- *Keep the time you are working with a small group short (15 minutes or so).*
  If you keep the group time short, you can more easily expect the other children to be successful working independently.

- ***Don't label the children by having permanent low, middle, and high groups.***

  Sometimes your small group time can include children with varying needs, and other times you will want children with similar needs to be together. For example, if you wanted to gather a few kids together so you could more easily observe how they did a particular task, or if you wanted to teach an activity to a small group which they would then do independently, you would want a heterogeneous group. If you wanted to work specifically with children having trouble with one-to-one correspondence or children who needed to work with number combinations of six, you would call the children with those particular needs together.

- ***Work with small groups only when you have a specific need, rather than having a permanent schedule.***

  It is important to think of the various classroom organizational structures as tools to use for different purposes when we need them. This allows more flexibility than setting up a permanent schedule that then dictates what we do and how we do it. For example, if I were to form four permanent groups who were to work with me one day a week, I would be focused on what I was going to do with each group for their block of time rather than on how I might meet the needs of my students as they became apparent to me. If I form small groups only when the need arises, I would be able to work with a small group of children who were having trouble with a concept for three days while the rest worked at independent activities. Another time, there might be a group of children ready for a challenge who could meet with me only once and be ready to work on that challenge independently. At other times, I might want the whole class working together for a few days on something, and I wouldn't want to work with small groups at all for a time.

Establish a Routine for Working with Small Groups

On those days when you plan to work with a small group, begin the period by gathering the whole class together on the rug. Remind the class of what they will be working on at the independent stations and that you will be working with a small group and should not be interrupted.

Ask the group of children you want to work with to stay on the rug. Give them a task to do while they are waiting for the lesson to begin. I often just let them work with the chalkboards, writing or drawing whatever they want. Other times I might give them a particular job like, "Count and write as many numerals as you can starting with 25" or "Choose a numeral you need to practice writing" or "How many ways can you write equations that add up to 7?" Excuse the rest of the children a few at a time to choose where they are going to work.

Watch the class for a few minutes to make sure they have the materials they need, know what they are supposed to do, and are settled in.

Work with the small group for 15 minutes or so. Then dismiss them to choose an independent station for the rest of the period or have them stay where they are and practice a task you just taught. Go around the room and interact with the children who have been working independently. Make note of any needs you will have to handle either with the whole class, in a small group time, or individually. When work time is over, ask the children to clean up and gather back on the rug. Spend a minute or two reviewing how the math time went, pointing out what went well that allowed you to work with the small group or discussing any problems that arose. This routine works even without other adults in the room. However, if you do have an aide or parent volunteer, he or she could monitor the individual stations, asking children questions while you work with the small group.

Teaching for Understanding

PART 4

Once we have established the routines and procedures for math time, we can focus on what is most important: the teaching of math concepts. This requires us to consider what it means to teach for understanding and to look closely at our interactions with our children and at our expectations for their learning. When our focus is on how children perform rather than on their understanding, we tend to teach children simply what to do or what to say. We create ***illusions*** of learning that we often view as success but that in fact mask children's lack of understanding. For example, young children can impress us with their ability to count by tens. However, this is not always as meaningful as we might assume. This becomes all too evident when we see children who are willing to count a pile of objects by tens, or ones, or fives, moving one object at a time as they say whatever sequence they are asked to count by.

"Ten, twenty, thirty..."

All of us remember times when we also didn't "get it," even if we were able to perform processes or memorize procedures. We learned to say the right words, but we didn't quite know what they meant. There was a level of insight, an "aha," that was lacking. On the other hand, when we (and children) truly understand a concept, we don't just imitate a process or follow a procedure. Understanding means we make connections and see relationships. We "get it."

What is

obvious to us is not always obvious to children.

If we watch children and ask questions of them to find out what they understand, we become aware that what is obvious to us is not always obvious to children. As we work with children, we also find that we cannot force children to understand. As is true for all learners, children must construct understanding for themselves. They need to go through that process of "getting it."

As we consider what it means to teach for understanding, it can be helpful to reflect on two states of mind we have all experienced as learners. Piaget described and labeled these states of mind as **equilibrium** and **disequilibrium**. When learners are in a state of **equilibrium**, they believe they understand something and are quite comfortable with what they know: they are not actively thinking or trying to figure anything out. However, when something happens that causes them to be surprised or unsure, then either they withdraw from the situation or their brain begins an active process of trying to figure it out. Their brain becomes actively engaged in a search for understanding. When what we are experiencing contradicts our previous understandings, when we feel unsure, puzzled, surprised, even confused, we are in **disequilibrium**. This is not undesirable; rather, it is the most opportune time for learning. Our brain wants to return to a state of comfort and a sense of knowing and understanding, and so is motivated to make sense of what we are experiencing. We want to figure it out.

The way we interact with children during this process is key. Helping children make sense of concepts requires very different kinds of experiences and very different kinds of interactions than does the kind of teaching that asks children to memorize answers and procedures that have no meaning for them. We can't force children to understand, but we can get them engaged in trying to figure things out by setting up situations and asking questions. The key is to get children thinking.

We need *to engage children in trying to figure things out.*

I am reminded of an experience a teacher once shared with me. She wanted her children to compare jars and determine which jars held more and which held less. She brought in several mustard jars that were the same shape but different sizes. Her students (six- and seven-year-olds) were distracted by the shape of the jars and predicted they would all hold the same amount of rice.

The teacher and the children then proceeded to check out their predictions. They first poured one jar into another to see what happened. Then they counted the number of scoops it took to fill each of the jars. After that they poured each of the mustard jars into a calibrated jar to measure how much each one held. When all the experiences were finished, David, one of the young students, said, "Well, I see it. But I don't believe it!"

Even
experiences can't always make us understand.

Confusion
is a natural part of developing understanding.

It is
important to know what children don't understand.

This story reveals two important principles about teaching for understanding. First, it points out that even experiences can't always convince us or make us understand. We see that even when we give children experiences, we can't assume that they have learned from the experiences. It is another reminder that what is obvious to us is not always obvious to children. It's not what they see, but what they understand about what they see, that makes the difference. Second, we can see by David's comment about his experience that he is trying to make sense of what he is seeing and not just trying to figure out what the right answer is supposed to be. His comment reveals that his teacher is interested in what children are really thinking and understanding and encourages them to share their thoughts. The children are comfortable enough to be honest about what they do or do not understand and don't feel a need to pretend to understand if they don't.

Confusion is a natural part of developing understanding. If we look back at our own learning, most of us will remember periods of confusion, of not quite getting it, as we worked to figure something out. These periods of confusion or incomplete understanding are not only natural, but often even necessary. The fact that children become confused or don't fully understand is not a problem or cause for concern. What can be a problem is our **lack of awareness** of their misconceptions or incomplete understandings. If we assume children understand when they don't (for example, if we never ask them to show us what they understand about counting by tens), we will not provide appropriate experiences. If we know, however, what children's misconceptions and incomplete understandings are, we will be able to provide what they need and will not assume they understand concepts they do not yet have the maturity or experiences to understand.

What does this tell us about our teaching if even experiences don't get the point across? Does this mean we just let children leave an experience thinking whatever they want to think? Not at all. Rather, it means we have to remember that understanding cannot be a one-lesson objective. Understanding develops and deepens over time. When a child does not understand, it means he or she needs more experiences working with the idea. David was not convinced yet, but this experience was still very important to his learning. He is in a state of disequilibrium and will remain engaged with this problem for as long as it takes to make sense of it. His interest in the problem has been stimulated. He will begin to look at jars more closely and ponder what is going on. He will continue to think. The teacher's responsibility is to make sure he has these opportunities and will continue to confront what he does not yet understand.

Children are much more capable, powerful, and confident when they are allowed to make sense of things instead of trying to follow someone else's way of thinking. It is important, however, to understand that allowing children to make sense of ideas in their own way does not mean we stand by waiting for children to learn. Rather, we must be clear about what we want the children to know and understand, and we must provide every opportunity for the children to come to understanding. Because understanding is achieved through the direct personal experiences of the learner, our job is to give the children appropriate experiences in which they encounter, interact with, and think about important mathematical ideas. We stimulate the children's thinking about their experiences and focus their attention on the mathematics by posing problems and asking questions.

If we truly want to teach for understanding, then we need to know what children **really** know and understand, not just whether they have learned to follow directions. We need to know what they **really** think, not just what they think they are supposed to say. If we want to teach for understanding, we need to know how children

Understanding
develops over time.

Children
need to make sense
of things for
themselves.

We need
to stimulate
children's thinking.

develop mathematical concepts and learn to recognize when they understand or do not understand. The more aware we are of how children think, the more likely we are to provide the kinds of experiences that support their search for meaning and understanding. We need to find ways to "see" what a child is thinking.

How Can We Find out (Assess) What Children Understand?

How children think is not always visible to adults. Children can learn to do a particular task in a particular setting, leading us to believe that they have a broader understanding than they do. We assume they will be able to apply what they know in other situations. Often, we assume children know more than they do because they can learn to use words quite effectively without understanding what those words actually mean. On the other hand, children sometimes are unable to express in words their understanding of concepts that they do in fact understand. We need to find ways, then, to assess more than the children's answers and uncover the thinking behind the answers. Much of the most useful information we can get about children's thinking is necessarily inferred from their actions and comments made while they are engaged in mathematical tasks. If children are encouraged to make sense of their work for themselves, they will share what they are really thinking instead of trying to read the teacher's face for a clue to the answer the teacher is looking for. We can then get the information we need by observing them and interacting with them. It is then that instruction and assessment can happen simultaneously and we can interact appropriately with the children.

Tasks that can be approached in a variety of ways will reveal more about children's thinking than tasks that must be done in a particular way.

We must

uncover the thinking behind the children's answers.

Consider the following examples.

Children Making Patterns

Approach One: A group of first grade children is learning to interpret a rhythmic pattern with materials. The teacher wants all the children to feel successful, so she tries to make sure they all do the task correctly. She begins a rhythmic pattern and the children join in: clap, clap, clap, shoulders, clap, clap, clap, shoulders, etc. She then leads them through the process of translating the pattern step by step. "How many times did we clap?" When the children respond with "Three," she directs them to get three tiles that are all the same color. She goes on to say, "How many times did we touch our shoulders?" The children respond "One." The teacher then tells the children to chose one tile that is a different color than the first three tiles. She continues to lead the children to make their pattern longer by using these same colors as she claps the pattern for them. If she sees that any child makes a mistake, she or another child helps them fix it.

Because the teacher set up this task to prevent errors, the task gives the teacher very little real information about the children's understanding. All she can see is whether or not the children can follow the directions and do this particular task. She can't tell, however, what the children understand about interpreting and extending patterns.

Approach Two: The teacher asks the children to interpret the pattern in any way they wish, using whatever materials they choose.

The teacher gets a wide range of information as the children create their various patterns. Since there is not just one way to interpret the pattern, the teacher sees the diverse ways the children made their patterns and the differing levels of their understanding of pattern. She sees this as valuable information because when she knows what they really understand, she does not make assumptions and has a better idea about what they need next.

There is another benefit to this approach as well. When teachers ask children to try to make sense of a task, the children are actively engaged and thinking in a way that does not happen when they are being directed through a task. This approach supports a search for meaning and understanding. Following the teacher's directions does not.

The teacher's responsibility does not end here, however. Once she sees what the children need, she must provide additional experiences, focusing the children's attention on critical ideas. During this particular lesson, she will have those children who made a correct pattern share their work with the others. Seeing several different models will help some of the children understand the task.

The teacher will also continue to provide additional pattern activities, surrounding the children with a variety of experiences over time.

Let's consider another example of two contrasting approaches to the teaching of the concept of measurement.

Children Working with a Measuring Task

Approach One: The teacher shows the children how to measure yarn by lining up paper clips. She emphasizes that they must be sure each paper clip touches the one before it. As the children work, she goes around and makes sure they are all doing the task as she directed them.

When the teacher looks to see what her children are doing, she can see who followed directions, but she cannot tell who understands measurement concepts and who does not.

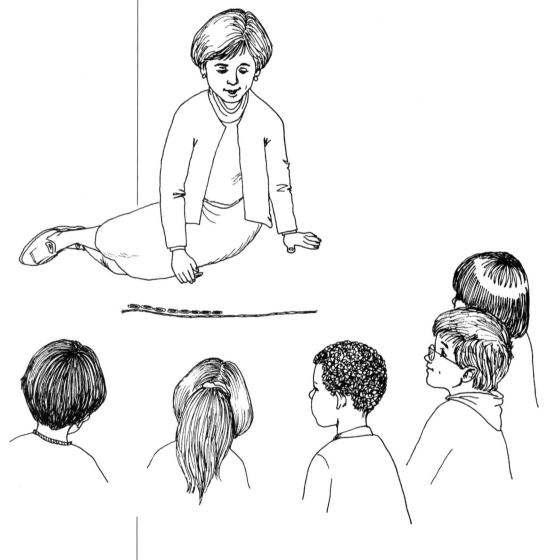

Approach Two: This teacher presents the task to his children by simply asking them to figure out how long the yarn is using paper clips.

The various levels of understanding are revealed in ways that would not be possible if the teacher had directed them through the task.

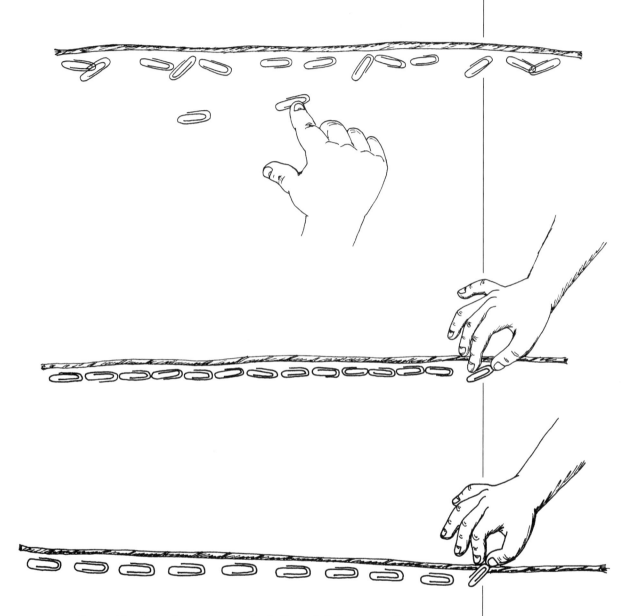

Once the teacher sees what the children really know and understand about measurement, he can then provide appropriate experiences. He can ask questions, focusing the children's attention and engaging the children in considering important aspects of the task.

In this case, instead of just telling the children that the paper clips have to touch, he interacts with them in the following way:

> "How many paper clips long did you find your yarn to be?"

> "When Bobby measured the yarn, he used more paper clips than you did. Why do you think that happened?"

> "Did you and Bobby measure the same way?"

> "What's different about the way you measured and the way Bobby measured?"

> "Do you think you could fit more paper clips along your yarn?"

> "Do you think you will get the same number of paper clips every time you measure?"

Some children will still not understand why it is necessary to have the paper clips touch when measuring. They will not be in a state of disequilibrium if they are not yet troubled by the differing results. They will be satisfied just to accept the results as they stand. However, asking children simply to follow directions and perform the correct procedure does not deal with their lack of understanding either. This only temporarily creates the illusion that they can measure correctly.

Finding out what children really know should be viewed as a successful experience even when it provides evidence that the children **don't** understand. If we view children's lack of understanding and/or misconceptions as failures for ourselves or our children, we will want to prevent these failures and make sure the children do things exactly as we showed them. However, if we view a lack of understanding as part of a natural learning process that we want to be aware of, we will give children opportunities to work in ways that reveal what they actually understand.

Teaching
children to follow procedures without understanding creates illusions of learning.

No matter what tasks the children are working with, we can find out more about what they understand if we ask questions. The following are examples of the kinds of questions that will give you insight into their thinking.

"Are you sure?"

"How do you know?"

"Can you show me?"

"Do you think that will happen every time?"

"What happened?"

"Why do you think that happened?"

Notice that these questions are not geared to getting the child to repeat the right answer. Rather, they ask children to explain or show what they are thinking or doing. You can tell whether the questions you ask will get information about what children are really thinking by asking yourself, "Do I already know what I want the answer to be, or am I really curious about what the child is thinking?"

We need to value the time it takes to get to know our children. Finding out what children understand is one of our most important jobs. The time we spend getting to know our children is absolutely essential and will allow us to be much more effective as teachers because we will then be able to provide more appropriate experiences.

How Do We Deal with Children's Errors and Misconceptions?

There is probably nothing more important when teaching for understanding than the way we deal with children's errors and misconceptions. We can have the right tasks; we can provide a positive working environment; we can give children manipulatives; but we will not support children's developing understandings unless we deal appropriately with their misconceptions. The challenge is to find ways to maximize children's learning without interfering with the child's sense-making process.

Ask yourself,
"Am I curious about what the children are really thinking?"

Our
challenge is to maximize learning without interfering with the child's sense-making process.

Children's work will have more value to them if they are allowed the time it takes to experience false starts, surprising results, and even some frustration. We must resist jumping in and interfering with the very process that can result in the most learning.

Sometimes a child makes a mistake that he has the ability to correct by himself. Often simply asking a question will get the child to reconsider and make the necessary changes. (It is important not to question children only when they are wrong. They should have opportunities to explain what they did even when they are right and should not assume that they must be wrong just because the teacher asks a question.)

Consider the following example: The child has made a design and described it using the symbols "5 + 2 + 1."

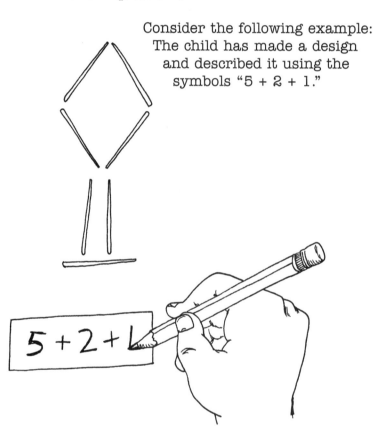

The teacher asks a question that gets the child to look again but also allows him to explain. (It is important to ask for the child's explanation, because sometimes the child is thinking about what he or she did in a different way than the teacher and is not actually wrong. In other situations, the children's explanations help the teacher understand what the children are having trouble with.)

"Where do you see the 5?"

In this case, the child responds, "Oh, I made a mistake."

The teacher still asks the child to talk about what he did to make sure the child is not fixing his work simply because he thinks the teacher wants him to.

"Why is that a mistake?"

The child responds, "Because there's only four there."

The teacher still does not tell the child how to fix the error, but says,

"Can you make the number sentence match the design?"

The child adds one toothpick to the design and fixes the error by himself.

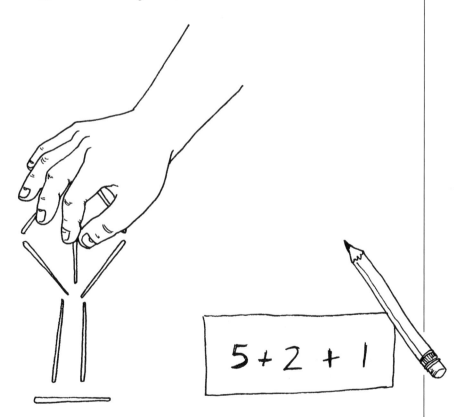

It is not always appropriate to help children fix their mistakes. Sometimes children's errors and misconceptions are the result of natural stages of thinking and understanding that children move through as they explore concepts and ideas.

The following example helps demonstrate this point.

> Karl organized a pile of lima beans into three groups of 10, with six left over. He knew immediately without counting that three 10s and six were 36. When asked how many he thought there would be if he counted them by fives, he thought for a minute and said, "55." His teacher asked him to check and see. Karl moved five counters at a time, counted to 35 and then counted the additional one and said, "There's 36." He didn't seem to notice that was the same number he had arrived at when he grouped the beans into tens and ones.

As surprising as this may be to some of us, thinking that the number changes when you count in a different way is a natural stage in children's development. Karl needs more experiences and more time to really know that the way we count does not affect the outcome. Some teachers would think Karl's needs would be met if they asked questions like, "Did we add any? Did we take any away?" Karl knows he didn't add any or take any away. What he hasn't quite come to terms with is that counting differently doesn't change the quantity. Teaching him to say "Counting doesn't change the number" will not enhance his understanding but instead can potentially diminish his beliefs in his own ability to figure things out.

Sometimes children's errors are the result of misunderstandings that occur because we ask children to perform tasks and procedures before they can understand them.

> When Lee was asked to find out how many beans there would be if he counted them by

fives, he moved one bean at a time, saying "five, 10, 15, 20 . . . ."

Lee has a misconception about what it means to count by fives. It is likely that this misconception came about because he experienced counting by fives as simply a rote process with no purposeful counting attached. Or perhaps Lee practiced counting nickels by fives, which reinforced his misconceptions. Even though Lee was able to count nickels correctly, the skill was taught prematurely. Counting nickels by fives **presumes** that one understands the idea that one thing can stand for many. When children count by fives before that concept is clear, it strengthens the incorrect idea in the child's mind that one can count lots of different ways and get lots of different answers! Lee's success in doing part of the task helped create the illusion that he understood what counting by fives was all about.

In order to deal appropriately with children's errors and misconceptions, we need to be able to distinguish between the kinds of knowledge that can and should be presented to the children and the kinds of knowledge that must be constructed in the minds of learners through their own reflections on their experiences. These two kinds of knowledge Piaget described as **social knowledge** and **logico-mathematical knowledge**. Social knowledge is information that must be transmitted by telling or showing. Logico-mathematical knowledge is knowledge about relationships which must be constructed in the mind of the learner.

Let's consider what kinds of knowledge children must possess if they are to solve a problem such as the following.

> Sara works at the ice cream store. A family came in and ordered two single-scoop ice cream cones, four double-scoop ice cream cones, and two triple-scoop ice cream cones. How many scoops of ice cream did Sara have to serve?

There are various errors a child might make when working with this problem. If a child doesn't know

Some mistakes come from a lack of information. Other mistakes come from a lack of understanding.

how many scoops in a single scoop, double scoop, or triple scoop, he or she could use the wrong numbers and come up with the wrong answer. In this case, the child is missing some **social knowledge** that the teacher should be responsible for providing. On the other hand, some children have trouble with this problem because they can't yet think about the various groups. They simply add up the number of cones and think that eight is the answer. In a sense, they don't understand the question and answer a different one that they do understand. When children can't do the problem because they can't yet think of four double scoops as eight scoops, two triple scoops as six scoops, and two single scoops as two scoops, they do not have the necessary **logico-mathematical knowledge.**

When we want to determine what mathematical problem solving a child can do, we need to make sure that the child has the necessary social knowledge to solve a problem and then step back and see what the child does with that information. If we try to help children be successful by leading them through the problem step by step, we will help them get an answer, but we won't be helping them develop the ability to solve the problem for themselves.

I think one of our most challenging jobs as teachers is deciding when to give information and when to accept the fact that the child will be unable to benefit from that information. If we consider it our job always to correct children's errors or to lead them to the right answer, we will often actually stop the children's search for meaning rather than support it.

The following examples present errors that children have made for many different reasons. The related discussions are intended to help us consider the best ways to interact with the children in these various situations.

First grader Stephanie was making up problems using Unifix cubes and story boards representing the park. She put out two red cubes to represent lady bugs and three black cubes to represent ants. She knew without counting that she had five cubes all together. On her small chalkboard, she wrote "2 + 3 + 5," which she read to her teacher as "two plus three makes five."

It is not too hard to determine that Stephanie has the required logico-mathematical knowledge to do the task with meaning, but does not know how to write this down in the conventional way. Stephanie's teacher was very comfortable telling her how to write the "equals" sign, and Stephanie confidently erased the "+" and replaced it with the "=."

I once observed another group of first grade children measuring the sunflowers they had planted. They were given meter sticks, and each was measuring and recording the growth of their plant. One of the children reported to me that his plant was 92. From my perspective, it looked about 3 inches (or about 7 cm) high. I asked the child to show me how he had measured. He took me over to his plant and showed me where he got the number he had written down in his book. The way he was measuring, the top of the plant did line up by the 92. The only problem was that he was holding the measuring stick upside down!

Let's try to figure out what information (social knowledge) and what understandings (logico-mathematical knowledge) the child lacked. Some would say the child lacks social knowledge, as he doesn't know how to hold the measuring stick right. They would teach the child what to do to prevent further errors. However, I would suggest that this error reveals the child's lack of logico-mathematical understanding. The child does not appear to understand what the numbers on the measuring stick mean. If he did, he would have been bothered by the unreasonableness of the 92.

He seemed to be doing what he was told because the teacher said to, rather than because he saw this as a way of recording the growth of his plant. I would rather have had the child cut a strip of paper the same length of the plant and glue that down on a piece of paper each time he measured. He could then look at the actual length of the paper strips and see how his plant was growing, rather than looking at numbers that have no meaning for him.

I observed a group of second grade children measuring jars to find out the number of scoops of rice that would fit in each jar. Their teacher had taught them that it was important to be accurate and had shown them how to level off the scoop by wiping across the top of it with a pencil each time they got a scoopful. Again, the children were more than happy to follow the directions. The only problem here was that the children were not really filling the scoops full (see illustration), and when pouring the scoops into the jar, they were not concerned when a fairly large portion of the rice in the scoop missed the jar! The teacher had provided them with a procedure they did not understand, which they used without understanding or effectiveness.

When working with children, we need to ask ourselves, "What does the children's way of doing this task reveal about what they know and understand?" It might seem reasonable to assume that the teacher should just explain more carefully to the children what being accurate means. However, I think their way of measuring indicates that they see no real need to be more accurate. The procedure of leveling the scoops doesn't mean anything to them or they would have paid more attention to that process. Children have to have a need to be accurate and some sense of what being accurate is about before a procedure intended to

What does

the child's way of doing the task reveal about what they know and understand?

help them be accurate can have any meaning. One way to get the children to consider the idea that the way you fill the scoops can affect the results would be for them to compare their outcomes. The teacher could point out that Peter got seven scoops when he filled the jar and Gina got eight-and-a-half scoops. Once they have the evidence that people can get different numbers of scoops for the same jar, they can be challenged to consider why that might happen. If that is a problem for the children (that is, if it puts them in a state of disequilibrium), they will begin to pay more attention to how the jars are filled, and the procedure of leveling off will begin to have more meaning for them. They then need to continue to explore the notions of "how close is close enough" and "how can I get closer" in a variety of different situations. However, if any of the children do not have the necessary logico-mathematical knowledge to be bothered by the discrepancy, they will simply accept the idea that sometimes people get seven scoops and sometimes they get eight-and-a-half scoops.

In another classroom, two children were working hard to figure out how many Unifix cubes long their rug area was. They were really excited to have measured and counted 428 cubes. In order to keep track of such a large number, they had broken the long train into sticks of ten. One of them came to me with several of the sticks of ten Unifix cubes to show me he knew another way to count them. "I can count these by fives, too," he said. He pointed to each stick of ten and counted, "Ten, fifteen, twenty, twenty-five . . . ." It may put you in a state of disequilibrium to think that a child can count correctly to 428, tell the number of tens he was able to make getting to 428, and still think he could also count the ten sticks by fives. But this is the kind of information we get when we listen to children. These concepts are more difficult than we sometimes realize, and children have much to sort out in their thinking about numbers. The fact that they think they can switch counting techniques calls into question the level of understanding they bring to the successfully completed task of counting to 428 by tens.

This misconception shows us several things: one is that the child has not sorted out what counting by fives means; another is that he seems to think that the way you count can change the number you end up with. You may want to question the child on the spot to get him to think about what he is saying. You could ask something like, "How many cubes do you think there would be if you counted all these Unifix cubes by ones? What if you counted them by tens? How many would there be if you counted them all by fives?" Sometimes just looking again at the situation will allow a child to correct himself. He might respond, "Wait, that won't work!" But more often the child will hold these conflicting ideas at the same time quite comfortably. That means he needs many more experiences over time to arrive at true understanding.

There are several things you can do to support the growth of understanding. The key is to recognize that in order to understand, one needs lots of experiences over time. Understanding is not a one-lesson objective. It is all right to show the child what counting by fives means, but more importantly, you need to find ways to model counting by fives and other groupings in meaningful ways in lots of different situations with many varied materials with the whole class. (Usually one child's misconceptions are shared by others!) When you are modeling, emphasize that counting by fives means five at a time, counting by tens means ten at a time, counting by twos means two at a time. Another way to support the growth of understanding is to have children work with smaller numbers that are easier for them to think about. While all children need opportunities to experience counting by various groupings, individual children will come to understanding at different times as they sort these ideas out in their own minds.

We must recognize that children's thinking and understanding evolve. We must think of concept development as happening over time. Children's ideas change and become more complete and more logical as they gain experiences and as they

Children's thinking and understanding evolve.

mature. Undeveloped ideas and misconceptions are a normal part of the child's evolving understanding. We can't prevent these misconceptions by teaching children to say words or perform procedures they don't understand. When children hold misconceptions, teachers can often help them come to new insights by providing additional experiences that allow the children to look again from another point of view. They can provide opportunities for the children to consider, notice, and draw conclusions. It is by encountering an idea in different settings and in many different ways over time that generalizations begin to form. If we insist that children must always have correct responses for concepts they are not ready to understand, they must resort to rote memory of these correct responses, because they will not be able to make sense of the situations by themselves. When we try to teach children our way of thinking or our way of getting answers before they can understand, we only interfere with their sense-making process. They stop looking for their own meaning and instead look to the teacher to see if they are right or wrong.

Curriculum that is appropriate for young children acknowledges that children learn from their own experiences and allows children to make sense of those experiences in their own way. Mathematical competence develops in children who learn that mathematics makes sense and who learn to trust their own abilities to make sense of it. In a learning environment where children are thinking and trying to make sense of things, children can grapple with ideas they do not fully understand and can come back to problems again and again while they work to develop understanding. When giving a child a task or a question, we do not need to know ahead of time whether it will be out of reach or not. If we are willing to learn from the children's honest responses, we will be able to present ideas to them in all their complexity rather than oversimplifying them in order to ensure "success." Recognizing that children can ponder an idea before they can be expected fully to understand it allows us to challenge them in a way that we couldn't if we expected them always to be right from the adult point of view. For example, we

---

Encountering
an idea in different ways helps form generalizations.

Mathematical
competence develops in children who trust their abilities to make sense of math.

can ask children to consider which mustard jar holds the most if it doesn't worry us if they do not know. Or we can ask a child to work with creating different shapes with seven sides, as long as we do not have a preconceived idea of how many they should be able to find, and as long as we know that they needn't be successful in order for the experience to have value for them. When they focus on making sense of situations rather than trying to figure out what the teacher wants them to do, children will not only reveal misconceptions, but will also surprise us by their ability to figure things out if we simply allow them to do so. Considering something they don't fully understand will be a problem only if we make children feel they are not good at math, or if we make them memorize words to explain something they really don't understand.

What Kinds of Records Should We Be Keeping?

As we broaden the mathematics we present to young children and focus on developing understanding, we need to find alternative ways to assess and keep track of their growth. Rather than checking to see if children have learned to perform particular procedures satisfactorily, we need to look at stages of children's developing understanding of concepts and at growth over time. We need much more information than a grade or a number can provide. One way that intermediate-level children present their growth in mathematics is through portfolios of their work. The portfolios contain the actual products that the children make as they work with mathematics. An important element for intermediate portfolios is that the children themselves choose the work that goes into the portfolio.

If we use portfolios in primary grades, we must recognize that they cannot be defined in the same way as they are at the intermediate level. For a primary portfolio to be a picture of what we know about children's growth in thinking and understanding, it should include the teacher's observations of the child at work as well as the results of individual interviews. It is extremely important that the emphasis not be on products produced by children. The young child's most important work is not going to appear on paper. It comes, rather, from engagement in activities. While children's beginning attempts to put their thinking down on paper can be of interest, their products do not reveal what is most important about their developing understanding. Putting too much emphasis on children's production of products can take away time needed for active involvement with tasks. And doing tasks primarily because they lend themselves to products that can be put in a portfolio is the wrong basis for choosing the experiences to give children. We need instead to plan experiences that support the development of the mathematical concepts we want our children to work with and then observe and make note of our children at work.

What Can We Learn from Children's Writing?

Many educators have embraced the process of writing about math as an important way for children to reflect on and record what they are learning. While it is true that putting thoughts down can be an important tool for clarifying thinking and can also give teachers valuable insights into student's thinking, we must think carefully about what this means for the young students we are working with. Learning to write about one's experiences is a valuable and timely process for young children, but there are several reasons why writing during math time may not be as valuable for K-2 children or as informative for the teacher as one might think. First of all, the children are still beginners at expressing their thoughts. It is a big enough challenge for most young children to begin to **talk** about their learning. **Writing** about what they are learning in mathematics, when writing itself is still a newly developing skill, can become a chore rather than an accomplishment.

The young child's most important mathematical work is not going to appear on paper.

Young children have difficulty reflecting on their learning and usually tell what they **did** rather than what they **learned**. They might say or write something like, "I worked hard with the geoboards. I made lots of designs." They are recording an experience, not learning more mathematics or clarifying their thinking about mathematics as older students might do. A math journal then becomes a diary of math experiences but does not enhance the learning of the mathematics. We see, then, that when young children write about math, it often is a writing experience and not a math experience. In a time period that is already too short, writing is not always the best use of the time devoted to the study of mathematics.

Because what young children put in a math journal does not typically reveal their level of conceptual understanding, the journal is not always a good tool for assessment. For example, a child may write about a measuring experience: "I measured the table. I used clothespins. The table was 24 clothespins long." We may find the children's spelling, ways of expressing themselves, and illustrations charming and more indicative of what the child can do in general than writing answers in a workbook would tell us. However, we still must look carefully to see whether or not this tells us much about their mathematical understanding. To determine what they know about measurement, we would need to **observe** the children **at work** to see how they measured, whether they measured in a straight line or not, how they lined up the clothespins, etc.

This is not to say that we don't want to provide children opportunities to write about mathematics. But we must keep it in perspective and not spend too much time or draw too many conclusions from what they are able to put down on paper.

It is important when we look at children's writing that we distinguish between a report of what was done and a record of the process the children went through. As children become more mature, they will begin to move from writing about the activity to writing about the process they used.

For example, when asked to determine the difference between 98 and 20, Sarah wrote about the process she used.

The table Sarah is 98 cubes long.

The trash is 20 cubes long.

The table is 78 longer

than the trash. ^{10} ^{10} ^{10} ^{10} ^{10} ^{10} ^{10}

I had 20, And I added 10 s till I got to 90, then I added 8,

Writing or drawing pictures can be a valuable and authentic part of a math experience, if it is a record of what the children discovered or accomplished. Children working with measuring jars by counting scoops of rice and scoops of beans wrote about what they thought about the experience.

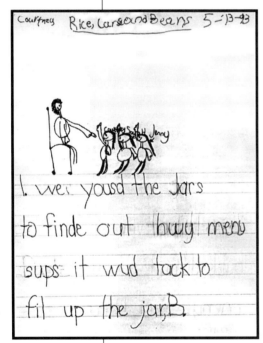

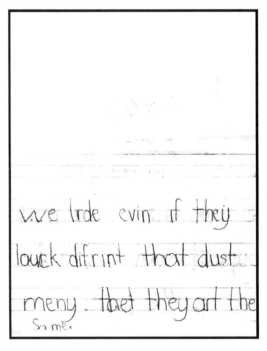

"We used the jars to find out how many scoops it would take to fill up the jar B. We learned even if they look different that doesn't mean that they aren't the same."

"I was surprised when I saw the measuring cup over flow 2 times. I was surprised when the rice was almost the same as the beans. Jar A was small. Jar F was big."

"We measured how much rice would go in each cup and which cup was bigger. I thought it would be D but it was C."

Although we want to provide opportunities for children to write about math experiences, we can help prepare them for the writing they will need to do in the future first of all by providing mathematical tasks that have meaning for them and that ask them to think — and then by giving them opportunities to share their thinking, **often** orally, and **occasionally** in writing.

Planning
for Concept
Development

PART 5

How Should We Plan for the Year?

*What About Investigations, Projects,
Children's Literature, and
Other Mathematical "Events"?*

How Do We Fit It All In?

How Should We Plan for the Year?

To make sure my program is balanced and all
major concepts are developed throughout the year,
I divide the year into three sections and make sure
that each concept is worked with in some way and
that ideas are revisited during each section.

	First 3 Months	**Middle 3 Months**	**Last 3 Months**
Creating the Environment	Explore materials. Establish working environment and procedures.	Explore any new materials as necessary.	Provide occasional opportunities to explore materials.
Number	Estimation. Acting out story problems. Begin number sense stations.	Estimation. Focus on number combinations. Write equations to describe situations.	Estimation. Addition and subtraction stations. Comparing number stations.
Pattern	Whole group work— rhythms, calendar, interpreting patterns.	Pattern stations. Interpret patterns with Unifix cubes, pattern blocks, tiles.	Re-experience pattern stations: add increasing patterns. Interpret patterns: add collections.
Measurement	Explore jars and rice and scales. Include measuring lengths and areas in number sense stations.	Direct comparisons— record results. Begin work with indirect measurement (units).	Continue to explore idea of a unit (using variety of non-standard units).
Geometry	Include reproducing designs in exploration time.	Create shapes from other shapes. Record. Explore properties of 3-D objects.	Sort shapes in a variety of ways.
Sorting	Pull out small groups to explore during exploration time.	Sort and resort a particular collection in a variety of ways.	Sort by given attributes.
Mathematical Events: 1 or 2 day experiences	Math and literature.	Data collection/graphing. Problem solving. Math and literature.	Data collection/graphing. Problem solving. Math and literature.

When planning for a year of mathematics, I consider number concepts to be the core of the program, so I establish ongoing work with number as the basis of the children's work. Other mathematical ideas lend themselves to a natural integration with this work with number. For example, measuring is a great context for developing number concepts and relationships. Data collection and graphing, which are ongoing activities woven into the math program all year, also support the development of number relationships. When children use dice in playing games, they have the opportunity to begin working with ideas of probability as they notice whether some numbers come up more often than others. Other major areas of emphasis, such as geometry, pattern, and sorting, can be interspersed for a week or two at a time throughout the year.

I have found that the independent work time gives the children the practice they need at their own level, so this is the most common way I have the children work. I think of the math program as moving from one set of related activities focused on a concept to another set of activities focused on another concept. The whole group activities are designed to provide children with the information they need in order to work well with the independent stations. The teacher-directed work with small groups of children during the independent time is to provide support, to challenge them or to gather information about their needs.

What About Investigations, Projects, Children's Literature, and other Mathematical "Events"?

I define a mathematical "event" as any experience that involves children in doing mathematics but that is not a part of any set of experiences that supports the development of a particular concept over time. The teacher chooses the task because it looks interesting and he or she thinks children will enjoy the challenge. Children's literature is often a source for these tasks.

Investigations can be another kind of mathematical event. While the term "investigation" can be interpreted in a multitude of ways, I am using the term to refer to any question that engages a child in a task to find something out. These special "events" can be interspersed throughout the year for a day or two at a time.

Investigations and other mathematical events can be an important part of the child's experiences with mathematics. They provide children with opportunities to see themselves as problem-solvers and to use the mathematics they have learned. We can often use these experiences to help us assess children's needs, as their approaches often reveal which concepts and skills they have internalized enough for them to be useful as tools and which concepts and skills they are not yet able to use.

Again, I have some words of caution. We must be careful to ensure that the use of children's literature and various investigations enhance the learning of mathematics rather than simply distract from the important ideas we want children

Mathematical "events" should not replace ongoing work with concept development.

to confront. We must be careful in selecting these experiences to make sure that the mathematical understanding gained is worth the time involved in doing the task. These experiences should not replace ongoing work with concept development.

How Do We Fit It All In?

This is an exciting time to be teaching mathematics because we are being encouraged to teach in ways that make sense to children. However, when we consider all that is involved, it seems overwhelming to try and plan for everything. We are urged to broaden children's mathematical experiences, to provide more problem solving, to connect math to the real world, to find ways to integrate math into other subjects, to make sure children are writing in the math classroom, to present math through children's literature, and to make math a part of long-term projects. The question is "Can we really do it all?" Or maybe more to the point, "**Should** we do it all?" It is impossible to do everything, so we must consider what will benefit our children most in the long run.

When planning mathematics (as well as other curriculum areas), we must take care to ensure that we are making the best possible use of our time. That doesn't mean we should rush and try to fit too much in. In a world where children are hurried from place to place, we need to create an environment where they are given time and allowed to focus, to think, to contemplate, and to learn. We do not want to underestimate the complexity of the ideas children must grapple with in developing an understanding of mathematical ideas. Children often need more time to work with an idea than we provide them. When we move children too quickly or too soon through experiences, they don't internalize or "own" the concepts they have been exposed to. Consider the numbers of fourth and fifth graders who are still counting on their fingers when asked such questions as "What is 14 + 9?" or who work

Children

often need more time to work with an idea than we provide them.

diligently to apply learned procedures to solve problems like 298 + 42. These problems could be simple for them if they had been given the time it takes to develop real facility with numbers and number relationships.

Remember, we are building the foundation, so giving children time to develop competence is important. We will never have as much time as we might want to work with mathematics. What we must do is choose carefully how we spend the time we do have.

In the long run, it is much more effective not to rush children through mathematical tasks and not to assume that simply exposing them is sufficient. They need experiences that have enough meaning for them that they can work with the ideas with some level of understanding (even if they don't understand fully). We do not want children working on ideas that are out of reach, thereby allowing them to be successful only for as long as they can remember what the teacher told them to do. We need to respect the real work of young children and not have them doing work that merely looks challenging and advanced but in reality is meaningless to them.

Trying to fit it all in should not be the goal. Choosing carefully and then giving children enough time to learn is the foundation on which good planning must rest.

Choose
carefully, don't try to "do it all."

Respect the
real work of the young child.

Some Final Thoughts

It really is possible to create a positive and productive learning environment that meets the needs of young children. There will still be challenges, difficult situations, and unexpected problems. Not every day will go smoothly. I have found, however, that the challenges are more easily met in an environment that truly is respectful of and consistent with how young children learn. Some of the unexpected moments will be quite wonderful: when the children groan because it is time to go out to recess and they would rather work on math, or when a child giggles with delight because he was able to accomplish a task that once seemed way too hard. Or even when the children clean up in less time than you were planning. (It really could happen!)

When creating the environment for learning mathematics, our goal is for all children to develop mathematical concepts in an environment that acknowledges and values each child's efforts to grow and to learn. In this environment you will see children working hard and working independently. You will see children engaged in tasks that have meaning for them. The children go beyond what you might expect. They have confidence in their own abilities to figure things out. This approach works and is effective because it makes sense to children. It engages them in thinking and working hard. It gives them opportunities to practice and to grow. This approach works because everyone can be successful.

Putting It into Practice

APPENDIX

Steps for Getting Started

Remember: You can't figure everything out ahead of time. So it's important simply to get started. Then you can look at where you are and consider what to do next.

1. **Gather the basic materials.**
   You don't need everything, but you do need to have enough materials to engage your class. Unifix cubes, toothpicks, and collections of things like shells, rocks, buttons, etc., can get you started.

2. **Plan storage for the materials.**
   You can create your own shelves with bricks and boards if necessary.

3. **Arrange your room to support an activity-based classroom.**
   Create a floor area large enough for the whole class to meet.
   Arrange tables or desks to make work areas for using materials.

4. **Plan activities and prepare the materials for a four- to six-week block of time.**
   The first one must be self-directed exploration. After that you will choose a particular concept to work on.

5. **Decide on the concept you want to teach.**
   What kinds of activities will you present?

6. **How are you going to organize your children for instruction?**
   Whole Group: Teacher-Directed Activities
   Choice Time
   Assigned Tasks
   Small Group: Teacher-Directed Activities

7. **Begin.**
   Give yourself permission to learn.

8. **Reflect.**
   What went well? What did not go well?
   What would you do the same again?
   What would you change?

117

Self-Directed Exploration

1. **Decide what materials you are going to introduce.**
   (You may want to include books, chalkboards, paper, and markers at first and gradually replace them with math materials.)

2. **Emphasize to the children that this is a work time.**
   Discuss what hard work looks like. Make your expectations clear:
   Share the materials.
   No throwing.
   Don't mess up other people's work.
   Clean up your work.

3. **Support the growth of independence and self-direction by reminding the children not to come and get you.**
   Reassure them that you will see everyone's work as you walk around.

4. **Observe the children at work.** Redirect any children that need reminding of appropriate behavior.

5. **Have something for the children to do as they finish cleaning up.**

6. **At the end of the period, gather together and briefly discuss how it went.**

7. **Expect the children to become more involved over time.**

118

A Math Time Routine

1. **Gather your whole class together on the rug.**

2. **Do a short activity (5-10 minutes) together.**
    This can be a mental math activity, an estimation task, a brief introduction to a new task, or a review of an old task. Remember to introduce new activities gradually, replacing the familiar activities with new ones over time.

3. **Remind the class of what they will be working on at the independent stations.**
    If a particular problem came up the day before, remind them of what you expect to see that day. If things went well, remind them of that.

4. **Excuse the children a few at a time to choose where they are going to work.**

5. **Watch for a few minutes to make sure the children have the materials they need, know what they are supposed to do, and are settled in.**

6. **Go around the room and observe and interact with the children.**
    Make note of any needs you will have to handle later with the whole class or in a small group.

    Don't expect it to be perfect. The environment you want to establish takes time.

    Allow children to work with any set of activities for at least four days before you decide it's not working. It takes time for them to settle in with something new.

7. **After the work time is over, ask the children to clean up and gather back on the rug.**

8. **Spend a minute or two reviewing how the math time went.**

©1997 Educational Enrichment   Math Time: The Learning Environment

A Plan for Working with Small Groups

1. **Gather the class together.**

   As usual, begin the period by gathering the whole class together on the rug. Remind the class of what they will be working on at the independent stations, and that you will be working with a small group and should not be interrupted.

2. **Ask the group of children you want to work with to stay on the rug.**

   Give them a task to do while they are waiting for the lesson to begin. I often just let them work with the chalkboards, writing or drawing whatever they want. Other times, I might give them a particular job, such as "Count and write the numbers starting with 25," "Choose a numeral you need to practice writing," or "How many ways can you write equations that add up to 7?"

3. **Excuse the rest of the children a few at a time to choose where they are going to work.**

   Watch the class for a few minutes to make sure they have the materials they need, know what they are supposed to do, and are settled in.

4. **Work with the small group for 15 minutes or so.**

5. **Dismiss the small group.**

   Have the children choose an independent station for the rest of the period, or have them stay where they are and practice a task you just taught.

6. **Go around the room and interact with the children who have been working independently.**

   Make note of any needs you will have to handle either with the whole class, in a small group time, or individually.

7. **When work time is over, ask the children to clean up and gather back on the rug.**

8. **Review how math time went.**

   Spend a minute or two reviewing how the math time went, pointing out what went well that allowed you to work with the small group, or discussing any problems that arose.

120

The Teacher's Role

The teacher's job is to help children develop a full and complete understanding (internalization) of the concept by providing many different but related activities. He or she supports individual children's growth by immersing them in (or surrounding them with) appropriate experiences.

The activities he or she offers children should
- Require children to think and look for relationships
- Have the potential to be experienced at many levels
- Have value in being experienced over and over again

The use of the activities should support the development of confidence and consistency as well as understanding.

Teachers need to challenge the children's thinking, helping them
- Make connections
- See relationships
- Confront their incomplete understandings

Teachers offer opportunities that help children
- Focus on particular ideas
- Make connections
- See relationships

However, teachers do not tell the children what to think. They structure the classroom so that what children really think and understand is revealed. They work with small groups and individual children,
- Questioning
- Observing
- Focusing the children's attention
- Modeling or presenting information

Math Time: The Learning Environment

What To Do When Problems Arise

- Treat the problems that arise as learning opportunities rather than as interruptions. (They really are!)

- Be honest and direct with the children. Remind them of your expectations. Don't assume that solutions or alternative behaviors are obvious to them. Discuss ways they might handle particular problems that may come up.

  For example,

  > What can you do if someone else takes the place you wanted to work?

  > What can you do if you run out of the materials you need?

  > What can you do if someone knocks over your work?

- Don't adapt the rules for the whole class just to accommodate one or two children who aren't able to work independently. Provide more guidelines for particular individuals if necessary.

- Instead of expecting everything to be perfect before you try it, just have an escape plan in mind. For example, if everything falls apart because you introduced an activity too fast and no one knows what to do, or you don't have enough materials after all, or the game doesn't work the way you thought it would and everyone is confused, don't panic. Just have the children clean up the math materials and then read a story or sing a song. You can reintroduce the task or choose another one tomorrow.

Dealing With Common Problems and Concerns

1. **Some children can't make a choice. They wander around and waste lots of time.**

    Some children need to check out all the choices first before really getting involved. If, after a day or two, they are still having difficulty making a choice, offer some help. You may limit the choices for them by asking, "Would you rather do this one or that one?" Just asking the question may help them decide on one you haven't suggested. If, on the other hand, they are still unable to make a choice in a reasonable amount of time, you may need to let them know that they are responsible for working hard and that you will make a choice for them if they can't do it themselves. Give them a chance the next day to choose by themselves again.

2. **Some children go to the same activity all the time. I don't think they are getting the experiences they need.**

    Children often know better than we do what they need to do, and they may be getting the experiences they need by repeating a particular activity. However, some children choose one particular activity over and over again because they feel comfortable there and know they can do what is expected. If you think the child needs to be encouraged to try something new, you might invite him or her to pick something that the two of you could try together.

3. **Because they get to choose the activity, some children think they are responsible only for having made a choice, and so they don't take the work seriously. They seem to associate choosing with free play and don't feel accountable.**

    We sometimes assume that children understand what we expect and are deliberately being uncooperative. It may be that we need to make our expectations more clear to them. Remind the children that their job is to work hard and that you are allowing them to choose so that they can find the job they are ready to work hard on. You need to let them know that you view this time as a serious work time and not as a free play time.

123

4. **Some children get upset because they don't get their first choice. Some race to get a place or refuse to choose because they didn't get to do what they wanted.**

   Often, children simply need reassurance that the choices will be there again tomorrow and that there will be other opportunities to get their first choice. Over time, children will see for themselves that they don't have to fight to get what they want. It helps children choose activities calmly if you dismiss a few children at a time to choose where they are going to work. Remind them that they should have an idea about where they want to work before they are dismissed, because you do not wait until they have picked a place before calling others to choose. Sometimes it helps to have the children "role play" the process of choosing so that they have a clear idea of what is expected.

5. **I try to provide a range of choices, but some children choose tasks that are too easy or too hard.**

   I have found that if I provide a range of choices, most of the children will choose the appropriate level. That allows me to focus on those few children who need more help or who need a challenge. After observing for a while to see how the child is working, I can determine whether the task is indeed too hard or too easy. I can then provide guidance if necessary.

6. **I just don't think kids are able to decide for themselves what level to work on. Many of my children will just do whatever is easiest. Other children will try to do things that are too hard just to keep up with their friends.**

   In my experience, children are able to decide for themselves what they need to work on if the classroom environment supports that expectation. However, in a classroom where children feel they are ranked or in competition with other children, some may respond by trying to do things that are too hard and others by giving up and doing whatever is easy. However, in an environment that values and supports each child's growth, this doesn't become the motivator. The teacher has an important role, not only in creating this environment, but also in observing children's needs so she can provide a challenge or help when necessary. Using "expandable" tasks makes this job easier than it would be if you had to provide a variety of tasks for a variety of needs.

7. **There is so much to deal with, I can't keep track of what everybody is doing.**

I have found that if I try to watch too many children at once, I don't really see anything. You will be farther ahead in the long run if you observe a few children closely. What you will find is that what you observe one child doing, you will notice other children also doing. There aren't really 30 children doing 30 different things. There are clusters of children working in pretty much the same way. You won't be able to (nor do you need to) take notes on every child every day. Just make sure you've focused in on a few children each day. Doing that will help you guide the class as a whole.

The particular individuals who really need you will make themselves known. This approach works because you are providing a variety of tasks that naturally meets a variety of needs and these tasks are available for children to experience over and over. The information you get from watching the children lets you know if there is some confusion you need to deal with or a challenge you need to present. Know that you will get better and better at picking up the clues from the children as you work in this way for a while.

Baratta-Lorton, Mary. *Mathematics Their Way*. Menlo Park, CA: Addison Wesley, 1995.

Labinowicz, Ed. *The Piaget Primer: Thinking, Learning, Teaching*. Menlo Park, CA: Addison Wesley, 1980: 107-108, 27-42.

McGrath, Kathy. *Working Levels* (workshop material for K-2 *Math Time* workshop, *Developing Math Concepts*). Norman, OK: Educational Enrichment, 1994.

National Council of Teachers of Mathematics. *Curriculum and Evaluation Standards for School Mathematics*. Reston, VA: National Council of Teachers of Mathematics, 1989.

Pengelly, Helen. "Acquiring the Language of Mathematics." In *Language in Mathematics*, edited by Jennie Bickmore-Brand, 10-26. Portsmouth, NH: Heinemann, 1993.

Richardson, Kathy. *A Look at Children's Thinking. Video I. Assessment Techniques: Beginning Number Concepts*. Norman, OK: Educational Enrichment, 1989.

———. *A Look at Children's Thinking. Video II. Assessment Techniques: Beginning Number Concepts*. Norman, OK: Educational Enrichment, 1989.

———. *Developing Math Concepts: A Supplemental Guide for the Developing Math Concepts Workshop*. Norman, OK: Educational Enrichment, 1989.

———. *Developing Math Concepts: Follow-up Study Guide*. Norman, OK: Educational Enrichment, 1993.

———. *Developing Number Concepts Using Unifix Cubes*. Menlo Park, CA: Addison Wesley, 1984.

———. *How Firm A Foundation?: What's A Teacher To Do? New Curricula for New Standards*. Washington: National Alliance for Restructuring Education and the New Standards Project, National Center on Education and the Economy, 1994.

———. *K-2 Grade Level Planning Charts*. Norman, OK: Educational Enrichment, 1995.

———. *The Learning Environment for K-2 Mathematics: What Does It Look Like?* Norman, OK: Educational Enrichment, 1995.

Richardson, Kathy, and Leslie Salkeld. "Transforming Mathematics Curriculum: Reaching Potentials." In *Transforming Early Childhood Curriculum and Assessment*, edited by Sue Bredekamp and Teresa Rosegrant, 23-42. National Association for the Education of Young Children, 1995.

WORKSHOPS

STAFF DEVELOPMENT VIDEOS

INDEPENDENT STATION CARDS

PRINTED SUPPORT MATERIAL

MANIPULATIVES

RESOURCE BOOKS

Available from:

Educational Enrichment
P.O. Box 1524
Norman, Oklahoma 73070
1-800-292-6022

Notes

Notes

Notes

Notes